# Healing Stress, Anxiety and Depression

Why your thoughts are killing you? Mental Health
Disorder, Mindfulness Meditation, Panic Attack
Relief, Managing Stress and Anxiety, Healing
Vagus Nerve, Vagus Nerve Stimulation

By

# Johann Burns

# TABLE OF CONTENT

Conclusion119

**4**

# Chapter 1: Introduction

She was a loner. But there are loners commonly found everywhere who like to spend time with themselves, but she was a different kind of loner – no interest in anything in particular, very hazy memory, not being able to make up her mind when required. She never slept well and even her waking hours were quite boring. She always felt hopeless; nothing treated her unexplained stomach upsets and headaches – even when there was no apparent lifestyle change that particular moment.

It was all quite mind boggling for the ones around her.

And then the worst happened.

She tried to kill herself.

And it was more than a usual death – it was death by depression.

Poor physique and depression induced overeating had already weakened her systems enough that her body could not even tolerate a mild overdose of sleeping pills.

Untreated, misunderstood and completely negative; she died a death nobody deserves. The people around her never got around to realizing that what she was going through might be a case of severe depression rather than her laziness, her eating disorder or lack of hobbies.

Have you come across somebody who needs constant motivation to remain focussed in life? Are you prone to mood swings that often end up in gloom and despair? Do your loved ones sometimes have aimless days and you feel your relationship deteriorating with time?

This, ladies and gentlemen, is depression – the dreaded enemy of today, and a reality of so many lives and even deaths. At some point of time we all feel sad, but momentary sadness is something and depression is something else altogether.

Depression is a disease, something for a clinically qualified healer and appropriate medicines can deal with, not something to snap out of or just forget about. Generally, it is the most underrated disease to which most people pay little heed and wait for it to go away on its own but it won't so a little more awareness and empathy is the need of the hour regarding depression.

This e book aims at providing a clear and comprehensive outlook towards this disorder along with discussions on impact of depression and the treatment as well. But first, we would like to congratulate you for picking this e book up so that there can be more scope for an open dialog with informed opinions.

We wish you a happy reading session.

# Chapter 2: Why Negative Thoughts? Why Stress?

Negativity unfortunately, has the power to destroy every nice thing in the mind of a person, and replace everything to be happy about, ever, with something nasty and upsetting. The more someone wants to get out of negativity, the more it grips them and consumes them and ruins their mood. A ruined mood leads to whole lot of complicated emotions and feelings of dissatisfaction. It leads to poor quality of life.

But what gives rise to these negative emotions and thoughts in the first place? What makes the mind get trapped in the sadness and ill-thoughts? Here is an analysis:

- There is a fear for the future

Negativity can rise from the perception of lack of control for something which hasn't happened yet. We fear what the future will bring. Since we have no idea about it, we tend to overthink. Overthinking about the uncertain can trigger negative emotions which tend to stick around. Though science has gotten very advanced with predicting the outcomes of short term, closed systems like elections, and scientists are continually striving to find even more accuracy in predicting nature, but the average person thinks about and worries about the future far more than its healthy, because of various insecurities. Many people try to be hopeful and positive about the future. They aim at never giving up, continuing their constant efforts but most fall prey to the disappointments and the kind of emotions the failures evoke. They fear failure and disasters. They keep on wasting energy on something which is not even there yet.

- There is worry about the present

They say what you have now is a present because you can truly enjoy the current moment. But seldom this present is capable of giving one peace and satisfaction. We worry incessantly about things which are happening beyond plan, things other people are doing, or not doing or something which might have happened unintentionally to us or our loved ones. This worry is an extension of another powerful negative emotions called fear. We are also in the throes of negativity because of forgetfulness, which leads to some mishap or the other. Today, in this world of information overload, there are so many things to remember within us or through our phones that the person is bound to forget something or the other. It is a highly likely phenomenon. But it continually leads to problems. There is anxiety and then eventual anger too, if our lives run at this complicated level. These things trigger a lot of negativity on a daily basis.

- There is shame in past

We all are knowingly or unknowingly carrying a lot of baggage from the past. We have all done things in the past which we are not very proud of. We have done embarrassing things. The shame that is associated with these actions can bubble up anytime, making us even more ashamed. This can make up brim with negativity. Such thoughts can drag us down in the murk, affecting our present even more.

Shame and embarrassment lead to hating self, even. If you stop liking what kind of a person you are, you might even stop being motivated to do the things you like. This pulls you even lower into the murk of negativity.

- There is a habit of overthinking

If you think too much, you think yourself into feeling more and more negative about even the small things. We are a creature of habit. If there is this habit which puts your mind into overdrive about everything, even if it doesn't deserve to be thought about too much. Actually, the mind-state can push you into believing the small little things which might be insignificant in the longer run, are worth too much of thought and need to be micro-managed. This is what leads to negativity. Consider this, maybe you bumped into someone on the road while carrying your mug of takeaway coffee and accidentally spilled over them, if you are an overthinker, this will simply drive you over the edge and ruin your mood completely with guilt. Overthinking can maximize that little speck of negative emotion into a monster of unreasonable proportions and eat up all the light from your soul. Also, since we are required to multitask at all times, it is mandatory that our attention is divided into too many things at one moment. This makes us anxious and may cause overthinking even the small things, losing peace of mind in the process. We are constantly distracted by too many things. This leads us to be impatient and causes negativity to set it.

- Emotions are our nature

Man is a unique organism. We have more emotions and emotional responses to various situations than any other organism, or se we can observe. There are complex emotions too, which are a by-product of our lifestyles. This can be a problem for our peace of mind and positivity.
Since we are also social, we are way too affected by what other's think or say or behave like. Their emotions in turn affect our own. they say feeling too much is also a problem.
We feel deeply and then we try to come up with a solution to restore peace in our mind.
Since the range of emotions which we can feel is high, the chances of it going wrong or troubling you is also very high.

- Thought energy can influence your state of mind

This is a slightly different concept from what the

usual, but haven't you heard, company which we keep influence us? The people around us can make us or break us by influencing our thought energy. The group which we go with around us, subconsciously shapes our thinking processes and also becomes a part of the voice of our conscience. These things pull us in a positive thinking or aa negative thinking direction. As esoteric it may sound, it is indeed true that our brain is actually an antenna to pick on vibes and if we are not careful, it begins imbibing those thinking styles to make its own. this is a phenomenon which can practically ruin your day and week because it will just begin rubbing negativity on to you and you will just absorb it. I'm sure you have noticed how meeting some people fills you with cheer and joy and being around some fills you with gloom and sadness?

These are the reasons why we feel negative at times. It is okay really to feel some things sometimes, it is natural after all. But if the emotion stays for a long time, refuses to go and affects every waking moment of yours, then it is probably something more of a condition than an emotion. You must consult a doctor for it.

**Why Stress?**

Little stress is great – it motivates you to finish the job which needs to be finished and get done with things like fine tune that report you have been meaning to send or run that last kilometer of the marathon. But if stress becomes a permanent thing, then you are not just on the edge all the time but also the body begins to show signs of stress via its functioning. It is not a great thing to be in stress all the time. There can be many triggers to stress, but the main reason is the guilt of not being able to handle the expectations of whatever is at hand or being scared of failing in it and the social anxiety that comes along with it. This negativity gives rise to stress.

Here are a few triggers, in which work related stress tops the list.

- Unhappiness in the work you do.
- Too much responsibility at work, much more than you can comfortably handle.
- Having no say in work decisions or not being clear in work expectations.
- Long and tiring work hours.
- Dangerous work and / or insecurity of job.
- Needing to talk in front of colleagues or unknown people continually as a part of the job especially when one is uncomfortable in public speaking.
- Discrimination, insensitivity, harassment, exploitation or any other business malpractice which one needs to face helplessly.
- Gender based wage gap at work.
- Loss of job.

- Life stress like death of a loved one, separation, childlessness or being parent to a special-needs child.
- Illness chronic or long – term.
- Financial pressure from family.
- Accident or mishaps.
- Marriage, readjustment or moving in with partner.
- Moving houses via purchase or rent.
- Taking care of a chronically ill family member, new baby or elderly family member care.
- Natural or human disaster, violence or other trauma.
- Overthinking or worry related stress like fear from uncertainty for things beyond control, like climate change, natural disasters, over-expenditure etc.
- Change based stress like a major life event which needs you to alter lifestyle, habits and perspectives.
- Attitude and perception- based stress for things which have happened in life. One might think of a situation positively or negatively, and if one takes it negatively, they will be in stress.

- Unreal and utopic expectations from self or others also causes a lot of stress. If one doesn't understand that we are all human and tend to not be 100% perfect, they will perpetually be in stress as they have inhuman perfection performance standards.

Effects of stress are beyond what meets the eye. The body and mind suffer endlessly due to stress, hormone system goes for a toss resulting in variety of physiological problems, the nervous system also collapses sending a frenzy of fight or flight responses and imbalances cause syndromes, not just symptoms. Chronic stress might even be lethal.

**How stress leads to depression and anxiety?**

Stress has a profound effect on mental health. Chronic stress always keeps one on the edge. This can imbalance the hormones. This feeling of being overwhelmed often can tax the nervous and endocrine system too much. Frequent bad moods and anger flashes due to too much stress is the causative for emotional health problems.
Stress makes the body release Cortisol which is also called the Stress hormone. While a little of it is fine, as it keeps one awake and alert, triggers appetite, fills one with excitement and enthusiasm etc., too much of it along with reduced Dopamine and Serotonin (linked to feeling happy and content) and other neurotransmitters in the brain can have adverse effects. The continued 'stress mode' if not

reset can cause a lot of trouble – mainly, it will just wear your patience and positivity off, apart from serious bodily functions – the first out of which is the digestive system. Slowly other functions also diminish, and profound sadness, lack of drive to do even simple tasks or even hyperactivity to make up for the lack of drive can engulf the person. This can be the link between stress and depression.

The grey areas of the brain decrease in extreme stress and also in depression. The stress is of losing something or someone in life, and the inability to cope with that loss of some kind can result into depression. The process of loss and perceived loss can lead to anxiety. This can be the simplest explanation of the relationship between these things.

Another expression can be – people who are generally stressed do not actively take care of themselves. These ignored factors can ruin lifestyle and increase stress burden to a level that puts the person on to a major depression risk.

One has to understand the relevance of the small things in order to figure out how one can deal with the two together and come up with a lifestyle and thought process solution which can cater to both, without putting anything else on risk.

## Chapter 3: What is Depression and how does it impact our lives?

We all feel sad at times in life – a bad breakup or poor marks in exam or failing to do a job at the expected standards can cause sadness. The loss of a near and dear one or a change that's too tough on sooth living can be distressing. But depression is different. Depression is not normal unhappiness. It is a more profound and deeper sadness which refuses to go away or become better. There are other symptoms too, which go along with the sadness. But it is unfortunate that because of it not being taken as seriously as it should, despite effective treatment, it becomes a serious, even life - threatening issue.
One needs to understand the concept of depression in order to get the help that's available.

The definition of Depression, according to American Psychiatric Association is: "Depression (major depressive disorder) is a common and serious medical illness that negatively affects how you feel, the way you think and how you act."

Some other ways to speak about depression
may be:
- Intense sadness -- including feeling
  helpless, hopeless, and worthless --
  lasts for many days to weeks and keeps
  you from living your life may be
  something more than sadness. You
  could have clinical depression.
- Sadness, feeling down, having a loss of
  interest or pleasure in daily activities -
  these are symptoms familiar to all of us.
  But, if they persist and affect our life
  substantially, it may be depression.

Basically, it is quite normal to feel sad and
upset after some triggers have been set off
like loss of a loved one, reputation or
something you dread happens. But if the
period of grieving, feeling down or in general
negative is prolonged, then it starts to affect
normal life function and it can be called
depression.

### The Symptoms

The symptoms of depression can range from mild
to severe, and can be identified as follows:

- Feeling sad for no apparent good enough reason. A person with depression can begin to feel sad to the core for seemingly fleeting reasons. This also causes and goes along with in general bad mood, lack of spirit and not being able to engage with anything.
- The activities or things the person once enjoyed don't seem enjoyable enough anymore. There is a general lack of interest in things, especially noticeable with lower pleasure derivation from things previously relished.
- Food becomes an escape or something to just barely fill stomach. Appetite changes cause the weight to reduce or get put on unrelated to dieting or any other workout. The person with depression might begin eating too much or shun and skip it.
- Sleep patterns change. The person with depression might experience lack of sleep or begin sleeping too much. There can be unexplained sleep patterns too, like sleeping in the middle of a workday or not being able to sleep until the morning.
- Increased fatigue can emerge. The person with depression might feel overly exhausted just because of the mind overthinking on a

regular basis. There can be loss of energy and feeling sunk or unable to hold up physically.

- A person might begin putting energy in purposeless physical activity like wringing of hands or pacing up and down for no reason. This is observable by others. There might also be a slowing down of speech and movements. There can be seemingly strange tics like pulling hair, biting nails etc., while these can also be in the symptom umbrella for some other behavioural issues as well.
- A person might feel worthless or guilty for little things and sense of importance for self might be quite low. One might even be hating oneself to the extent of emptiness, zero self-worth and emotions pushing one to suicidal tendencies.
- It is difficult for the depression patient to make quick and sound decisions even for the little things. They face difficulty thinking and concentrating. They might be easily overwhelmed by little inconveniences rather than be able to manage them.
- The patient of depression constantly thinks about death and suicide. The thoughts stem from perceived worthlessness. They are nearly obsessed with death.

Depression can affect 1 in 15 persons in a year and 1 person in 6 have experienced depression at least once in a lifetime. These symptoms need to range for a couple of weeks to be declared depression. Being sad is not equal to depression. Sadness and grief may have some similar symptoms but in element they are different.

Points of differentiation might be:

- If one is in grief or just sad, there are waves of deep negative emotion which wash over the person rather than constant, numbing negativity or sadness for a good couple of weeks.
- In sadness or grief, the idea of self-esteem remains. There is no self – loathing or hatred as is observed in depression.
- Grief or loss or sadness can cause depression in some people. So, trigger to depression is grief but the reverse is not true.

Several risk factors play an important role in depression as a disease. They decide if someone gets depression or remains safe. It can even happen to anyone who lives in relatively ideal or good conditions!

**Risk factors**

- Biochemical factors, which can contribute to depression symptoms as the chemicals which are being released differently make the person more susceptible to depression.

- Genetic factors, which make the person susceptible to a disease much more and cause the metabolism to be such which doesn't really stop the disease.
- Personality factors which make a person who already has poor image of self and who are easily overwhelmed by stress more likely to experience depression.
- Factors of the surrounding, which make people who experience violence, neglect, poverty or abuse much more likely to experience depression.

Depression can be treated; it has accurate medication which can cure the patient successfully. It is one of the better conditions in mental disorders as about 80% of patients respond well to medication. If not being 100% better, the patient at least experiences better mood or at least better in terms of symptoms. The diagnosis happens after a session of talks with the psychiatrist or psychologist who try to quantify the patient's symptoms and place it in mild, medium or severe. Apart from intensity, the history of the patient, medically and otherwise, the nature of environment and quality of life the patient has is evaluated and accordingly the treatment imparted. Sometimes, a blood test might be required because depression might be linked to a physiological condition like Thyroid.

## Stages for treatment

The treatment can be done in three stages:
1. Support: discussing practical solutions to combat depressive state and the stresses that contribute to the feeling of negativity; also educating family members about the grittiness of the patient's situation.
2. Psychotherapy or Cognitive Behavioral Therapy: The patient is talked to about their thoughts and how they see things to reach at the root of the depression. For mild level cases, this is the only treatment which is imparted because it is capable of working effectively. For more advanced level of symptoms, the psychotherapy is used alongside other treatments, in conjunction to them.
3. Drug treatment for the condition: Using anti-depressants to combat the low and negative feelings associated with depression and other drugs to use to help suppress the symptoms. Usually, drug treatments are used for moderate to severe conditions and never prescribed to children. Even to adolescents and teenagers, these medicines are

prescribed with caution. These drugs can be selective serotonin reuptake inhibitors (SSRIs), monoamine oxidase inhibitors (MAOIs), tricyclic antidepressants, atypical antidepressants and selective serotonin and norepinephrine reuptake inhibitors (SNRI) which are used for a spectrum of neurotransmitters. Even if the symptoms have recovered, the drugs should not be discontinued as there is a chance of relapse. Sometimes, the drugs may increase or intensify the symptomatic discomfort for the first few weeks of administering them, but they must not be discontinued.

Other therapies include aerobic exercise like running and sport, which may assist with mild depression by stimulating the norepinephrine which is directly related to mood. If there is severe depression and cannot be treated by drugs or the patient does not respond well to medication, electroconvulsive therapy or ECT is very beneficial to treat psychotic depression.

Depression is treatable by various means and methods. Generally, depression is brushed off as a bout of sadness and with a wave of a hand people expect the patient to just feel better and cheer up – it actually doesn't work that way. The patient himself doesn't quite realise that they are going through depression but a correct approach towards mental health can improve the situation. One must distinguish sadness from depression, grief from depressive mind-state and avail the available help. There can be many types of depression too. They can be understood as follows:

1. Unipolar or Bipolar depression

Here, the depression can be associated with other factors as well. If the predominant feature is simply depressed mood, then it is unipolar depression. If along with perpetual poor spirits and sadness, there are bouts of good mood sometimes, and manic episodes too, it is called Bipolar depression. Often, Unipolar and bipolar depression is also conjoint with anxiety. Research shows that all individuals with bipolar disorder definitely have depression as well.

2. Psychotic depression

If the depression comes along with psychosis, like delusions, false belief and being far from reality, hallucinating or talking and believing things that do not exist is called psychotic depression.

3. Postpartum depression

This is a kind of depression which comes after the baby is born. The mother might experience some blues where due to hormonal imbalance; she is overly emotional, teary and hurt with small inconveniences, but postpartum or postnatal depression is more severe than just 'teary' or 'upset'. It can be as severe as the mother wanting to hurt the baby or even murder the baby to put an end to her misery.

4. Major depressive disorder with seasonal pattern

This kind of depression was previously called SAD, this kind of depression occurs due to reduced sunlight in a particular season, affecting the hormones in the person which are responsible for feeling happy and contented. The depression stays for just that time, lifts for the other seasons when light is appropriate. The countries where winter is long and severe, this condition is quite prevalent.

**Depression affects quality of life**

Depression is all consuming. It affects the quality of life deeply. Here is how:

- Depression affects normal bodily functions and requirements even so the patient of depression cannot even eat or sleep in peace. The appetite changes, sleep patterns alter, ruining routines and causing physiological changes.
- Depression fatally affects the way the person interacts with other people. Usually, a social stigma sets in. since depression makes the person teary or very sad even at the slightest triggers, they might refrain from meeting, talking to or seeing anyone. These ruin the social life of the person. All this coupled with the lack of will to do anything forces the person to shun all contact with others.

Sensitivity towards judgement from others makes it tough for them to tolerate as much as an untoward glance in their direction and can feel offended and triggered.

- Depressed people cannot make decisions properly. Even seemingly small and simple decisions like what to do after getting up can be overwhelming and they might stay in bed all day simply because they cannot decide what to do next. This has profound repercussions because simple things become demons and hinder with normal living.
- People with depression are not motivated to do anything. This might even be something as simple as taking a bath. People with mild depression can be a troubled lot at work because they are never able to perform at optimum level in the workplace.
- Depressed people are fatigued all the time. This interferes with anything they want to do. This has far reaching impacts on daily life because if there is utter lack of energy in the first place, coupled with lack of motivation, it is too much of effort for the depressed person to actually end up doing.

# Chapter 4: Why people opt to take their lives?

Suicide is one of the most common reasons of death in the US, with 45000 people killing themselves in 2016 and the rates rising every year. It is alarming to see developing country citizens finding life tough to a level that they don't want to live it anymore, despite the obvious perceived comforts and conveniences.

Depression is a big cause of suicide all over the world, and there is strong link between the two. At the root of half the number of suicides, depression is there. Here are some reasons why depressed people want to kill themselves:

- The loss of hope

There is a complete loss of hope in a depressed person. There is not much to look forward to. There is general hopelessness and more so, from self. This negative spiral of despairing about the moment to come can be lethal literally, as it can fill the person with extreme loss of will to even continue living. Since in depression, this condition of loss of hope happens, it can be traced to the pressing need to end life when someone is in chronic depression.

- The only way out

A depressed person is constantly suffering because of the perpetual sadness they experience. Since they cant find anything to pull them put of their misery, nothing which excited them before seems to be making them happy anymore and since the world seems to be conspiring against them, the only solution to put an end to the misery comes across in the form of suicide. If there is no life, there won't be any suffering is the central theme.

- The chance at a better existence

Since the quality of life of a depressed person is quite poor, they are convinced that there cannot be anything worse than their life itself and maybe by ending it, they will get a better chance in the next lifetime.

- Because it seems simpler than just dealing with the discomfort of depression.

The thoughts of killing oneself bring a lot of clarity in an otherwise muddled up life of a depressed person. It gives a purpose and sense of perceived achievement which motivates a depressed person to begin working towards.

- Because the reason for the depression can only be eliminated if one's life ends

Suicide comes across as an answer to the very reason why the person is depressed actually. It may be an irreversible situation like death or something which has the person trapped. A depressed person is not capable to think of ways to bounce back from a situation and falls into the negativity. Eventually, after struggling for a long time, the perspectives are so lost, it is impossible to track back and find help – killing oneself looks like the easiest and most permanent and convenient solution to the problem at hand.

- Everyone is better off without me

A person battling depression is always sad, and they also realise how it affects the people around them. They feel like being an emotional burden for everyone else, are extremely sensitive to how people react to their sadness picking on even the smallest reactions whether intentional or unintentional. They end up feeling as if they are ruining the party and it will be better for everyone around them if they stop existing anymore.
A depressed person might not openly be vocal about their intent to end their life, but even by little and superficial observation, one can figure out the tell-tale signs that they are gearing up for a suicide plan.

**The Signs**

Here are a few signs to look out for:
- They are researching death topics, how to kill oneself, talking about it openly and dwelling on the subject too long. These are the direct signs to be careful of. But studies show that this is not very common. Most people with

suicidal tendencies do not let others know and just do it out of the blue.

- They are becoming even more withdrawn with time. They isolate themselves, with no friends of theirs around and no communication with family.
- They are making plans like updating their will or getting rid of stuff or writing a note.
- They show despair and hopelessness of their life openly. They might talk about pain or being a burden.
- They are showing extreme swings in mood, becoming reclusive and sad and then turn calm when they have decided to go through with the suicide. They can be moody, irritable and anxious. They can be angry and upset even. Then be tranquil about the situations next moment.
- They may begin to act very recklessly, as if they hold no value to their life or wellbeing. They might start drinking too much, doing drugs, having unsafe physical relations, drunk driving and the like.

All the signs of suicidal tendency must be taken seriously. Help can reach in time and a life can be saved if these behaviors are taken care of in time. If a person with depression has had a history of attempts to kill themselves or have had near and dear ones commit suicide, or have had a traumatic event in the past, they are in high risk of attempting suicide again.

The myths about suicide in depression, like if they are causally talking about it they won't go through with it, they are saying or doing something just for attention, if that's what they want to do what can I do, they really want to die, one mustn't talk about it because why put ideas in someone's head – all these need to go away. It is not like a depressed person relishes the thought of killing oneself, but due to their mental – emotional condition, they are unable to see how it is no the best way forward. They need help not judgement. If one can help people with depression and suicide, one must because it is a matter of one invaluable human life.

# Chapter 5: How to Identify Depression?

While there is nothing palpable about depressed people, you may have to be alert and notice changes in a person's behaviour to determine whether he or she may be suffering from this disease. Usually, some or most of these symptoms need to be manifested almost every day for almost two weeks for it to be considered a depression.

- Energy Level Fluctuation

It is seen that people who are tending towards depression are often low on energy levels. They may often feel sluggish and lazy. These people would put off physical activities and they will hate it if you pressurise them to exercise. The fatigued and sluggish outlook may convince you that a person is depressed especially if even simple tasks take a lot of time to complete.

- Concentration Issues

Depression is often characterised by problems in concentration. It takes increased effort for people to focus and make the right choice. Decision making gets affected so the rational mind takes a beating. One also tends to forget things and this can be detrimental in the long run.

- Irrational behavior

Being depressed is like taking a ticket to the land of irrationality and making reckless decisions. Taking un-calculated risks and putting oneself in harm is one of the dumbest things that people who are depressed resort to. Hence, a lot of depressed people turn to substance abuse to derive the feelings that they think they have lost. Other activities that they could resort to, include gambling, gaming, driving, or bungee jumping. The rush of adrenaline that accompanies each of these activities is perhaps what gives them solace.

- Change in Body Weight

Both, eating too much as well as eating too less are real signs of depression. One may start binge eating to counter the emotional after effects of depression and this could lead to tremendous gain of weight, Often, this is because comfort eating calms the brain in ways that normal food cannot.
Loss of weight is another after-effect or symptom of a depressed mind. One simply stops eating or begins to cut calories in an unhealthy manner.

- Loss of Interest

When a person's interest in hobbies and pastimes goes for a toss then it is an indication of something being very wrong. The hobbies in question might be simple things like reading, writing, drawing, sketching or painting. If a person who swears by photography suddenly loses interest in capturing the rarest of sights, then it can astound all.

Depressed people go out of the way to avoid things that can make them happy and they stay away from joy. It appears as if they feel that they do not deserve any happiness and hence shy away from situations that might force them to experience it.

- Change in Sleep Patterns

Our sleep can tell a lot about our mental situation; depression is evident when insomnia sets in. As your mind is too busy processing incidents and analyzing repercussions your sleep can take a massive turn. Many people who are sad also tend to sleep more than the normal sleep hours if they are said to be depressed. This is especially true of youngsters these days and the cause of depression is often the breakups. This habit of sleeping more than required is called hypersomnia.

- Self-loathing

During instances when depression is caused by loss of a loved one or because of a certain traumatic incident, one can develop very strong feelings of self-hatred. Sometimes it is also called survivor's guilt and people who are afflicted with this cannot stop criticizing themselves for their perceived faults and errors. A lethargy and restlessness sets in that keeps reminding you of your helplessness and this in turn makes you vulnerable to suicide or other such extreme actions. A person may have recurring thoughts about ending his/her life and will need to be closely monitored by the people around.

- Temper Issues

A depressed person usually has temperamental issues. Anger can cause even the best people to be mean and unreasonable. The tolerance level of a person goes for a toss and it may seem like violence may be the only way forward.

- Feeling of blah-ness

When there is an air of despair and hopelessness, it feels like the world is a dark place, all bleak and dreary. People often complain of pains that may seem rather irrelevant at first but slowly they begin to have different meanings. It can be a simple stomach pain caused by over eating or you could be reeling from having exercised too much (aching muscles and body pain in general), when you know that you do not deserve to get an ache but you do have one, then it may be because you responded positively to the test of depression.

# Chapter 6: Combating Depression

## Medications

There is a wide variety of antidepressants that are available in the market that help cope up with depression. These work on the brain chemicals called neurotransmitters such as serotonin and norepinephrine.

Always take medicines for depression only after consulting with a physician and if you notice any side effects, then you must immediately report it to the doctor in charge. Generally, for the best results, you should take antidepressants for at least 4 to 6 weeks. Just because the symptoms start to fade away, it does not mean that you can stop taking the medication. Doing so will only make the problem return with a vengeance instead immediately stopping the antidepressants can cause withdrawal symptoms even though they are not addictive. According to studies conducted by National Institute of Mental Health (NIMH), people who did not recover after taking the first medicines increased their chances of combating depression when they started a new medicine.

But how drugs affect depression
Some chemicals can help change the hormone reception patterns in the brain, changing the way brain is working under stress.

1. Tranquilizers try to calm the body and ultimately the mind as well by blocking the signals brain in sending out to the body.

2. Selective serotonin uptake inhibitors change the levels of serotonin in the brain, stabilizing moods.
3. Serotonin norepinephrine re uptake inhibitors and tricyclic antidepressants alter moodiness and fill the mind with renewed energy and will to do things.
4. Norepinephrine dopamine re-uptake inhibitors help increase the levels of dopamine in brain, boosting mood.
5. Monoamine oxidize inhibitors help brain cell communication and increase all mood building hormones like dopamine, serotonin and norepinephrine.

Thus it is quite important to take medications regularly and diligently according to the doctor's prescriptions and also take care of the diet which is prescribed along with these drugs. It is not sufficient to just know about the drug you are taking but also to keep a track of mood changes and social behavior along with medication.

**Exercise Your Way Out Of Depression**

Your tummy might not be telling you to shed those pounds and your weight may be completely in control but that does not mean that you should not be exercising regularly. Getting out of bed may seem like such a difficult task but once you make up your mind, it will become an easy task. After going through some extensive research and studies, it has been found that depression and exercises may be more closely related than you ever thought. When you exercise, your body releases endorphins. These endorphins are chemicals that interact with the receptors in your brain, which in turn reduce the perception of pain.

The release of endorphins (feel-good hormones) causes a sense of euphoria, it is the high that a person feels after having gone for a run or an intense workout. In some cases, they may also act as sedatives, relaxing your mind and body at the same time. These chemicals are made in the spinal cord and brain and released in response to neurotransmitters. The effect achieved by the release of endorphins is the same as that of morphine in the blood stream. The main difference is that unlike the later, endorphins do not cause any addiction and you will remain independent of drugs.

The continued physical activity also triggers the growth of new cells in the brain that in turn increase mood-enhancing neurotransmitters. This relieves muscle tension, reduces stress and provides a general aura of well-being.

**So What Happens When You Exercise Regularly?**

The benefits of exercising regularly are known to all and it is proved time and again.

- With regular exercise of about 20 to 30 minutes each day, one can effectively reduce stress due to the emergence of endorphins.
- It makes a tremendous amount of difference to your sleep pattern. When you burn enough calories and tire your body out, then you will be improving your sleep.
- It helps to keep anxiety at bay because you are involving the bodily muscles into a strict and reinforced activity.
- A different sense of self esteem begins to boost your morale
- There is a lot of good that exercise does for your health – it keeps the blood pressure under control, improves muscle mass, strengthens bones, reduces fat and in general, makes you a fit and healthy person, ready to take on the challenges of the world.

Exercises are underused in eradicating depression. The benefits of moving about, burning calories, and lifting weights are that you will soon begin to fall in love with this period of sweat and strain because of the high that accompanies it. If, like me, you are a little unsure of your commitment to a cause, then it is a great idea to join an exercise group. Not only does it keep your resolutions strong, you will also enjoy the company that you have. Your social support group must consist of people who will inspire you to wake up and hit the roads with gusto.

You can team up with neighbors, your best friend, or even siblings and have competitions amongst your self. Joining an exercise class is also good as there will be more people and it will make a good place to socialize. Now what are the exercises that you could opt for?

If you are looking at outdoor activities, then opt for fun exercises like cycling, swimming, jogging, and brisk walking. These are great forms of cardio and they will go a long way keeping you in shape. All those who do not have left feet would do well if they joined dance classes or the other hip variants such as aerobics or Zumba.

If you like your exercises to have more stretch and flexibility, then Pilates or yoga would be your best bet. With consistent exercises and a healthy attitude towards life, you will battle away the depression blues in no time.

Exercises do not necessarily mean that you have to hit the gym and do a strenuous workout everyday. What you basically need to do is get some activity done, getting up, moving about, and doing chores i.e. small adjustments to your lifestyle that could have lasting results on your waistline. If you have a dog, then start walking the dog after dinner. If your workplace is situated in a multi- storeyed building, then start taking the stairs instead of the elevator. Challenge yourself to remain on your feet throughout the day and you are sure to see some good results.

## Follow a Healthy Diet

A healthy diet is essential for an individual's physical and mental well-being. People suffering from depression often take to binge eating and drinking in order to cope up with their situation. Although it may provide some temporary relief, it will harm you in the long run. Lower your sugar intake and avoid eating processed and junk food. Switch to a better diet and incorporate healthy fruits and vegetables in your diet. If you don't know what diet you should follow, you can consult a dietician and start a healthy diet.

Usually people opt for comfort food when they are going through an emotional turmoil. Foods such as ice cream, cake, and chocolates increase serotonin, a chemical in the brain that uplifts mood. These foods are high in sugar and carbohydrates and although they may help you feel relaxed and calm when you are depressed, it will cast a negative impact on your body in the long run. If you consume junk food on a regular basis, it will increase the risk of obesity-related diseases, such as diabetes and heart problems. It will also make you prone to heart attacks. Apart from this, you will gain weight, which might turn out to be another cause of depression. Therefore, instead of gorging on cholesterol-rich products like chips and pastries, you should add low-fat dairy products, fruits, vegetables, and whole grains in your diet. While some people may eat a lot when they are depressed, some others eat too little which makes them weak and prone to sickness. It is understandable if you don't find the strength or motivation to eat when you are depressed and feel low but if you keep skipping meals, it will worsen your condition. You have to make an effort to consume at least two meals a day. If you don't feel like eating full meals, you can opt for your favorite fruits and vegetables. Make a simple sandwich with lettuce and cheese and eat it. It doesn't require much effort and will also fill you up. Remember that avoiding food will not help you in any way. You will feel irritated and your anxiety levels will increase if you skip food on a regular basis.

Some people avoid food because they don't find the strength to shop for food items and cook. In such cases, people usually eat whatever is available. For example, if there's a pizzeria in front of your house and you don't feel like cooking, you might end up eating pizza every day. This can cause serious health issues and will only worsen your depression. Some people also fall into the pattern of eating the same food every day. For instance, they may go on a diet of cereals and this will not be beneficial in any way. You should eat five different types of vegetables and fruits every day along with whole grains and protein-rich foods. If you don't feel like going out and purchasing grocery items, you can order them online. Make a sandwich or stir fry some vegetables to make a quick meal.

Food plays a significant role in our life and you should always follow a healthy diet. Add variety to your diet and avoid binge eating. If you feel like eating something even after you have had a full meal, you should stop and ask yourself if you are really hungry; don't use food as a mood stimulant. If you want to soothe your mind, opt for books, music, or movies instead. Consult a nutritionist and talk to them about your condition. Seeking professional help is always a good idea when you are undergoing depression.

**Get Rid of Negative Thoughts and Feelings**

Your thought process plays a significant role during the time you are depressed. It is very easy to get into a self-hating or low esteem mode when someone is depressed. If you continuously keep thinking about your past and how you couldn't do anything to change it, you will get even more depressed and slowly your mind will be lost in a dark abyss.

In many cases, it has been observed that people get depressed when their relationship fails. You might think that this is the end of the world and you won't be able to live a normal life again. But, this is just not true. Time is the best healer and with a little patience and effort, you will be able to recover from your depression. If you think you can't get your mind off something, distract your mind. You can read a book to divert your mind. If you have been avoiding your friends and family, call them up and go out with them. Think of something that you like to do. It could be anything from dancing to watching movies. You can ask a family member or a friend to accompany you. This way you won't feel lonely and it will also motivate you to start a journey of self-discovery.

You have to stop negative thinking if you want to battle depression. Sometimes people get depressed when they have to deal with the death of a loved one. For example, if you are a mother who has lost her child, it is undoubtedly the worst time of your life. Especially if your child died in an accident or was a victim of a fatal disease, you might not be able to forgive yourself. You should know that this is not your fault and you have done everything you could, to save your child. If you keep thinking about such things, which have triggered your depression, you will not be able to heal yourself ever.

Fill your mind with positive thoughts, tell yourself that you are a fighter and you deserve to live a happy life. Go through your old pictures when you were happy and recollect the amazing times that you spent with your loved ones. If you can't think of anything that makes you happy, seek professional help. You can take help from a psychiatrist and talk to them about your condition. They are trained to listen to you and to help in your battle against depression.

Changing your perspective towards life will go a long way in fighting depression. When you stop thinking negatively and start looking at the bright side of life, you will learn that there is always a path to happiness, only if we are willing enough to search for it.

# Let Go of Your Past

A lot of people fall victim to depression because they cannot let go of their past. Sometimes young men and women cannot move ahead with their life because of infidelity and failed relationships. What they fail to understand is that we cannot change our past, but we can change our present and build a happy future. If you have faced something similar in life, don't hold onto your anger and resentment. Imagine yourself being bound by thick iron shackles and you are unable to free yourself because you are not thinking about the solution but focusing only on the shackles. You will be able to free yourself only when you look away from the shackles and search for the key. Here, the shackle is your depression and your key to happiness lies in forgiving and forgetting.

You have to ask yourself if you are happy by staying stuck in your past? Are you doing anything valuable or are you contributing to the society by not moving out of your past? NO. When there is no positive outcome of holding onto your anger and sadness, why not let it go?

Let go of your grudge because it is not helping you. If you can't get the thoughts out of your mind, write it down in a journal. Writing will help you express your feelings and will also make you feel lighter. If you don't feel like writing, talk to someone and share your thoughts with them. Focus on the good things in life. Try to remember how much your family loves you and how your friends text you every day because they are worried about you. Your present is worth more than your past and the more you try to focus on your present, the happier you will feel.

Imagine yourself carrying a ten pound weight on your head. Now think of what happened in the past and how someone hurt you so much that it wounded you deeply. Next, think about all your blessings and privileges. Does one person or one incident change the meaning of your existence? No. Now forgive yourself, forgive that person, and forget about that incident. Slowly imagine the ten pound weight lifting from your head. You are feeling lighter and happier. Your mind is free and you are a happy person now. Do this mental exercise in your mind and it will definitely help you feel better.

If you want to battle depression, you have to let go of your past and start focusing on the present and future.

**Talk to Someone about Your Depression**

Talking can be really helpful when you are fighting depression. Usually, people shut themselves from the outside world and stay lonely and alone. This will not help you in any way because the more you think about your worries and sorrows, the more you will plunge into depression. If you don't feel like socializing or meeting too many people, try talking to someone you trust. It could be a family member, your cousin, or a close friend. Remember that the people who love you will never judge you. Don't feel humiliated or embarrassed about your situation. You would have helped someone out too and so you deserve to be helped. Discuss your issues and ask them to listen to you. Sometimes, just being able to share your worries will help you feel better and lighter. Many people suffer because they don't have anyone who would listen to them. So, if you know someone whom you can trust, call them up and ask them to come and meet you.

On the other hand, if you are not comfortable in talking to someone you know or you think you can't trust anyone, consult a psychiatrist. Often people avoid visiting the doctor because they think nothing is wrong with them and they don't need to go to a psychiatrist. Every mental health issue is different and needs separate treatment. Don't think that seeking medical help for your depression will affect your normality as a person. People shy away from visiting a psychiatrist because they think the society will judge them and that they might not be considered normal. You are absolutely normal and you are just trying to be happy. Everyone deserves to be happy and if it requires professional help, so be it.

The treatment for depression varies across different people. Some people cope up with depression with the help of antidepressants and medication. However, you should never try to take antidepressants all by yourself. Self-medication can be dangerous and it may do more harm to you. Sometimes antidepressant medicines have to be chosen based on your other physical ailments. Some medicine will not work in people suffering from heart or liver disease. Also, you are unique and your medication will be unique too. What works for someone else might not work for you. So, how do you take medication for your condition? Consult a doctor!

Psychiatrists have the expertise and experience to treat patients suffering from depression. They will be able to analyze your condition correctly and will prescribe the correct medicines. This way you will know that you are taking the correct medication. Apart from medicines, psychiatrists also use talk therapy to treat people suffering from depression. During a talk therapy, you will just discuss your problems with the doctor and they will listen to you and provide solutions for your problems. This kind of treatment has proved to be helpful for a lot of patients and generally people feel lighter after being able to talk about their depression.

The treatment for depression can range from simple medicines to electric shock therapy depending on the patient's condition. However, when the first sign of anxiety and sadness sets in and if it prevents you from doing regular activities, you must see a doctor. Don't be scared that you have to go through complicated treatments and large doses of medicines. They are just a part of your treatment and in the end you will be benefited.

## Start Your Life on a Fresh Note

Before you start reading this part of the book, you should know that you are an amazing person and everyone loves you. Let's assume you were a popular face in your college and everybody looked up to you. Whenever you got on the stage to perform or give a speech, people applauded and cheered for you. Can you recollect those happier times? What has changed now? You are still the same person if you remove the bad incidents from your life. So, why should you stop living a normal life? Everyone deserves to be happy and you are one among them. Even if you were not the college rock star or you were never popular among your peers, you are still loved by some people and that should be motivation enough for you to start living your life again.

When people are depressed, they can't see their true potential and ignore all their achievements. If you are going through something similar, you should learn to see the best in yourself and think about how your parents were proud of you and how your friends bragged about your success to others. You should find the motive to live your life happily again. If you keep feeling low and anxious, it is not going to make you happy. Find your purpose in life. For example, let's say you are a professional dancer and you have won several dance championships. Find your love for dance again. Go through your costumes and watch your dance videos all over again. Watch yourself transform into an amazing dancer on screen and see how people were mesmerized by your talent. Make it your goal and start dancing again. Go back to your practice sessions and begin focusing on this one thing. The more you shift your focus towards something that you love, the more you will be able to get out of depression.

Don't try to focus on too many things at the same time. Your mind is overworked and concentrating on too many things may leave it confused and perplexed. Just think of one thing that you want to do. It may be anything from doing well in your career to going for a vacation. Put all your strength and energy into that goal and tell yourself that you have to complete your mission.

Rejuvenate yourself and find your self-worth again. You have the right to enjoy an awesome life and only you can make it great. So, start working towards your goal from today and don't let life's troubles stop you.

# Chapter 7: Knowing Yourself and Your Emotions

They say charity, cleanliness, and in general any good deed begins at home. Similarly, the path to wisdom doesn't start at some Ivy League university or fancy school; it begins right at your home – yourself. But not many of us know what knowing ourselves actually means. Read on to know more about this.

## Why is Self-Knowledge Important?

Knowing yourself transcends beyond knowing just the physical and materialistic aspects related to you. It refers to being touch with your psyches, your emotions. There are many reasons why knowing yourself is extremely important. In fact, some of the reasons are unique and especially important to some people. For those who have lost someone close to them, knowing their weaknesses can help them overcome them at a time when despair threatens to engulf everything. For those who have been through a traumatic time, knowing oneself can help them avoiding doing things they know will affect them negatively and remain strong to charter a new, improved course of their life.
Here are some other examples of why knowing ourselves is important on a general basis.
1. Happiness – When you can express your feelings in an appropriate way so it gets

meaningfully heard, you feel lighter and happier with yourself. Your grievances can be remediated only when you voice them, you get things when you ask for them. And when your problems are solved or when you get the things you want (they may be materialistic or intangible in nature), then you definitely feel pleased for voicing out.

2. Peace with Self – When you do things that go against the grain, at least according to you, then you feel anxiety, agitation, guilt, frustration, anger – and a host of other negative emotions. But when your actions are in tandem with your personal decisions and beliefs, you feel at peace with yourself. It is important to know what you want in order to do that which avoids inner conflict within yourself.

3. Improved Decision-Making Skills – People who don't know themselves don't know what would make them happy, what is right for them, or even what they actually need in order to survive. And this habit to dither over making a decision can impact even the simplest aspect of your life to the most important ones, such as deciding what you want to order at a restaurant or deciding whether your partner is the right one for you.

4. Enjoyment and Vitality – The periods of indecisions, anxiety, guilt, frustration, and anger that you face when you have not made the right decision, or are unable to make one can ruin your personal and professional lives. Most people don't believe it, but your inner turmoil does show on your face. Over a period of time, they carve lines on your face visible to all in addition to scoring your soul which only you can feel. But when you are sure of who you are and what you want, you feel a sense of purpose and vitality that is unbeatable. You have a more focused approach to everything and enjoy your challenges rather than rue at them.

5. Self Control – A smart person knows that temporary gratification is not worth the after and side effects that the means of achieving it cause. People who know the mistakes they make, especially those who take short cuts in their life, can avoid making them by exercising self control. Instead of indulging in bad habits and decisions, you start making conscious efforts to make good ones. Building your willpower to say no or sticking to right but difficult paths can happen only if you learn to overcome the things or avoid those

people & situations that impair your judgement.

6. Handling Social Expectations – What many of us don't know is that there are times we do unconsciously things simply because the society dictates it, whether we like or not. Don't believe it? Here's an example. It's that time of the year when your efforts for the past 10-11 months are evaluated and you are either given a raise or reprimanded for your mistakes. Around this time, your boss whom you detest because he has a very negative and challenging attitude throws a party. The only things bigger than his fancy sedan is his ego, so you're in a dilemma. Your natural instinct is to avoid going to any part organized by a detestable person but because you can't afford to miss his party because everyone else is going, you too end up going there. But if you know what your feelings about it are, and what your reaction would be after you go to such a party, you would avoid getting into such a situation. Sticking to your values will help you to always say when that's what you want to say, not because social norms dictate you should.

7. Better Relations and Tolerance Power – Often, people pass judgements or make harsh

comments based on the face value of other people or situations. Not many people stop to think about what the other person may be going through. Not many people are cognizant of the fact that the other person is a human too, and as prone to make mistakes as one self is. When you know your weaknesses and acknowledge your faults, you learn how to think from the other person's perspective better; you empathize much better thus helping you make more tolerant and humane decisions.

Now that we know why it is important to know ourselves, let's look at aspects that are common. Managing these aspects, or VITALS, of ourselves will help us achieve the level of self-knowledge that will help us be better versions of ourselves.

### V – Values

Ethics such as being empathetic, or helping others, or achieving a certain position at work, or health, or maintaining financial security are just some values which act as driving forces of our actions, and therefore our actions. Here's a simple example: Let's say there are two people who work at the same place and each earns exactly $3,000 per week. But one among them is married with two kids while the other is a bachelor. Friends at work have planned for a 3-day vacation, colleagues only.

While the driving force behind the bachelor may be relaxation and adventure, the driving value of the family man may be adding as many dollars to his kids' college funds as possible. So we know what their decision would be. The bachelor would be more likely to join the friends while the married person would feel happy because he has added more the bank account. Both are right in their place because each one's value is different. Knowing what values matter to you help you make decisions that support your values. Even when you are tempted to do something wrong, or give up after many failures, your values will help you stay determined, and build a positive frame of mind to stick to your path and achieve your goals. Those without values are like ships without a compass. They may travel from one point to another, but they don't know which direction they're going, what pleasures or dangers lie before them.

### I – Interests

Hobbies, passions, indulgences, or any activity or person which draw and retains your attention over a long period of time can be termed as your interests. In order to find out what your interests are, you need to ask yourself a few simple questions.
- What captures your interest?
- What things cause you concern?
- What things are you keener to learn about?

When your mind is anchored by a fixed goal in

your life, it makes you passionate about achieving it. Know what interest you help you understand your deeper passions. Let's look at another example. Let's say you are employed as a software tester. It is your job to ensure the software codes written by our developer colleagues are working as expected. But what really captures your interest is knowing how a code is written, and how it unfolds when commands are entered by a user in the system. What this implies is your passion is not finding issues with the code, but to lean how it is written, to unravel the mysteries of computer software and probably build one yourself. There are many other examples of people making their interests the biggest successes of their lives, entrepreneurs being fantastic examples of this category.

### T – Temperament

A simple definition of temperament is inborn preferences combined with natural instincts. Are you more productive when you work alone or in a team? Do you feel more comfortable when you're alone (an introvert) or happiest when you're surrounded by people (an extrovert)? How do you take criticisms from others? Do you have to plan your every move or are you okay to go with the flow? Are you comfortable taking on big challenges or do you prefer making small conquests? Are you prone to make decisions based on facts and thoughts or do you trust your instincts more? The responses to these questions makeup your temperament profile. These will also help you to make the right choices so you prosper rather than make decisions that cause you harm.

## A – Activities

The activities referred to here are more to do with your daily habits, or around-the-clock activities rather than the ones you perform sporadically. Some of the points that fall in this category are – are you the early to rise early to bed type of person or do you prefer staying up late in the night and complete your work? When do you feel the most active? Defining such things help you plan your major activities accordingly and ensuring you succeed because you are comfortable with the way the activities are conducted. Following your internal clock is a manner of respecting yourself, your personal makeup. The process of defining the pace at which you like working is known as defining your bio-rhythm.
Here's a simple example. Say you have started hitting the gym. You prefer a light warm-up exercise for the first 20 minutes before you start lifting weights and doing other strenuous exercises. But there are a few people who hit the road running. 5 minutes in and they're doing push-ups and dead lifting weights. If you were to try to match their pace and vigour, you'll tire yourself out. Moreover, if your gym partner were to have completely different schedules from you, you don't

give your 100% to the activity. Have a like-minded gym partner will motivate you to exercise for a longer time and with more confidence, so the session would be more productive than painful. Remember – it's always easier and more fun to do things that define you, rather than trying to be someone you're not.

## L – Life Goals

Sometimes, defining life altering goals can depend on how you let important events in your life impact and shape you. When you ask yourself about the most meaningful and important moments in your life, you will know what things matter to you most. You will find a common thread amongst all of them that will help you define your driving force. For people who have faced challenges repetitively and have risen to the top, the value they cherish the most could be self-reliance, persistence, and hard work. These values will help them define their next course of action, and thereby define the goals they want to achieve in life generally.

## S – Strengths

When we talk about skills, they need not just be skills, talents, or knowledge. They can also include characteristics such as respect, humility, and curiosity, sense of fairness, love, loyalty, and gratitude. When you know what your strengths are, you can make them the reasons for your self-confidence and positivity. When you focus on your strengths, you are encouraged by compliments and don't let unfair criticism affect you too much. You become a sponge for the "good" and try to use your positive skills to do something useful for yourself and others.

# Chapter 8: Depression and Anxiety

Several people experience both depression & anxiety several times, often at the same time. Losing a job or a loved one, divorce, illness, grief, and several other factors, also known as stressors, cause negative emotions such as frustration, sorrow, worry, and loneliness. Believe it or not, these are natural coping mechanisms that almost every person experiences at some point in their lives.

There are however a few people who experience these stressors on a daily basis, without having a reason to do so. Due to this people lose the ability to perform even regular activities such as being punctual for appointments, meeting deadlines at work, self-care & hygiene routines, sleeping, or even caring for children and other family members. Such people are either struggling with depression or anxiety or sometimes both.

There are studies that prove that between 10% and 20% adults during any 12 month timeframe visit their regular physician when they suffer from episodes of periods of depression or anxiety disorders. Out of such people, almost 50% of these people have symptoms of co-morbid, anxiety disorder or secondary depressive. The presence of both depression and anxiety at the same time, also known as co-occurring emotions, is mostly a chronic condition amongst more people than you can think. Such people also have additional disadvantages due to this complex condition – they take much longer to recover, and the instances of suffering from these episodes happen on a recurring basis along with psychosocial disabilities.

## The Relationship between Depression & Anxiety

One of the most commonly asked questions is – can depression lead to a condition called social anxiety disorder (SAD)? Or is it possible for SAD to lead to depression – the reverse? There is in fact a very close relation between both these conditions, so much so that that they co-exist very commonly. It is in fact a very commonly asked questions by people who don't know the difference between the two and wonder what exactly is it they're suffering from, or are they suffering from both conditions. When you feel anxious because of every person or activity in your life, and you feeling tensed when you are out with people, sometimes even your own family, you tend to cut yourself off from everyone else and avoid participating in your usual activities. At the same time, few features of depression also result in you struggling with phobias from people and things around you for reasons big and small. Research has shown that generalized forms of SAD can also be linked to a spike in the chances of suffering from depressive disorder, post traumatic stress disorder, alcohol abuse, and panic attacks at the same time (known as co-occurrence).

## Depression Leading to Anxiety

While it is commonly known that anxiety can lead to depression, even the other way around holds true. At this point, it is important to know the difference between these two. Let's look at their symptoms in order to do so.
Major Depressive Disorder Symptoms
One of the key parts of major depressive disorder symptoms is a two-week period at which time a person is either in a depressed mood throughout the day for almost every day, or they may suffer from a loss of interest or joy from almost all activities in his life. Some of the other main symptoms linked to this disorder are:

a. Low self-esteem or inferiority complex

b. Bouts of acute guilt

c. Insomnia or hypersomnia (excessive sleep) almost everyday

d. Agitated psychomotor actions or retardation almost everyday

e. Substantial loss of weight even when one if not dieting, or rapid weight gain, or radical changes in appetite

f. Excessive fatigue almost everyday

g. Inability to concentrate on an activity for too long, and indecisiveness

h. Repeated thoughts of death, suicidal thoughts without any plan, or with a plan, or making suicide attempts

People suffering from major depressions have high risk of suffering from anxiety, social impairments, occupational challenges, and inability to function properly in other aspects too.

**Anxiety Disorder Symptoms**

With this disorder, the key factor is of course high levels of anxiety and excessive worrying over even the smallest activities or events. What's important to note here is that the level of anxiety experienced by the people is not in proportion to the chances of the unlikely event actually taking place. This level of high levels of anxiety can last for more days than not over a period of 6 months.
People suffering from anxiety and worry have at least 3, sometime more, of the below symptoms. These symptoms co-exist for a large number of days during the six-month observation period referred to above.

    a. Getting tired easily
    b. Irritability
    c. Disturbed sleep patterns
    d. Challenging to concentrate on things or blanking of the mind frequently
    e. Feeling keyed up or on the edge accompanied by restlessness
    f. Feeling of tension in the muscles

In order for the worry felt to be categorized as a disorder, the worry, anxiety, and physical symptoms should lead to major or complete disruption of social, occupational and general activities in life. There are other ways to distinguish anxiety disorder from regular, non-pathological anxiety. Here are some of them:

a. This form of worry lasts for a very long time
b. The intensity of worry is very high and generally always interfere with a normal life
c. This level of worry invades every part of the person's life, can easily be picked up by even casual observers or people not known to the patient, and causes a lot of distress to the person suffering from it
d. This form of anxiety is always accompanied by physical tells, like a nervous tic, which indicates being keyed up or restlessness

**Other Risks Associated with Depression & SAD**

If a person has both problems, the person is also more likely to struggle with other accompanying challenges due to this particular combination. The below related issues have in fact also been published in 2001 in "Primary Care Companion Journal of Clinical Psychiatry: Psychotherapy Casebook" and its studies:

1. A higher risk of struggling with alcoholism
2. Higher risk of committing suicide
3. Poor or no response to any treatment
4. Inability to perform normally in social and occupational settings

**More about Anxiety**

As mentioned before, anxiety in fact is a very
common emotion that most people experience,
some more than most. When anxiety is felt on a
regular and more intense level, it becomes a
medical disorder that leads to high levels of
nervousness, worry and apprehension.
Due to anxiety, a person's psychological as well as
physical behaviours get altered. Over a long period
of time, these symptoms get calcified into physical
symptoms, as mentioned earlier, such as excessive
sweating. Over 40 million people in the United
States alone struggle with anxiety disorders. It is in
fact the most common type of mental illness in the
nation. But the worrying part is that out of this
large number of people, just 36.9% approximately
receive treatment for their disorders.
According to the American Psychological
Association (APA) anxiety can be defined as "an
emotion characterized by feelings of tension,
worried thoughts and physical changes like
increased blood pressure."
Although obsessive compulsion disorder (OCD),
post-traumatic stress disorder (PTSD), as well as
acute stress disorder are no longer classed as
anxiety issues, there are still a few different other
types of anxiety that we need to know about:

   a. Generalized Anxiety Disorder – This type of
      anxiety involves excessive as well as long-
      term worries over indefinite life events,
      situations, and material objects. This is the

most common type of disorder and people don't often recognize it for what it is

b. Panic Disorder – Short & sudden attacks of terror usually form part of this type of anxiety disorder. The attacks often cause shaking, nausea, breathing problems, and dizziness. When panic attacks happen, they escalate in intensity very rapidly, usually after 10 minutes. But these attacks usually last for several hours. These attacks are usually triggered by scary incidents or long bouts of stress. But sometimes they also happen without any triggers. People who suffer from sudden, unexplained instances of panic attacks can read too much into the attacks and take drastic measures to avoid it or get away from it.

c. Phobias – This form of anxiety is an illogical fear of specific objects or situations, often leading people to avoid them completely during their lives. Unlike anxiety, phobias are different because they can be traced back to a specific trigger. People who suffer from phobias in fact almost always know they have an irrational fear but are unable to do anything about it. They cannot control the rush of anxiety they feel when they come into contact with that event or object. There are a wide range of triggers, such as animals, scents, sunlight, surprises, etc.

d. Involuntary Mutism – In this anxiety type, mostly associated with children, they are unable to speak at certain places or under certain circumstances, sometimes in school or when they are asked to do public speaking. They are however perfectly capable of speaking freely around familiar people, places, and in comfortable situations. This type of anxiety can be extreme in some cases.

e. Social Phobia or Anxiety Disorders – This type of disorder is usually associated with embarrassment in public or negative judgements from society. This kind of anxiety is displayed via a wide range of emotions such as fear of intimacy, and severe anxiety over possible chances of humiliation. In this case too, people usually avoid going anywhere near their anxiety triggers, thus stunting their social lives to a large extent.

f. Separation Anxiety – The apprehension a person feels when they are separated from a place or person they care about a lot is also known as separation anxiety. While we all experience it on a very low level, people suffering from an anxiety disorder feel the pain of their separation very intensely and react in unexpected and erratic manners.

## Depression Leads to Anxiety

As we've seen above, there are certain characteristics of depression which makes people isolate themselves from the world and avoid confronting their fears. Due to prolonged isolation and sense of unhappiness, it is possible for people to start developing anxiety disorders while they had none before that. There are have been several instances in which people who did not suffer from any form of anxiety first go through a traumatic experience which leads to severe depression. Because of the onset of depression, they also become plagued with SAD and a host of other psychological problems, usually co-depending on each other.

While depression is usually linked to a feeling of hopelessness and dejection, anxiety is more frequently associated with fear or worry. The problem is, when isolation and negative thoughts take a toll on a person's mind, they can lead to phobias which cause depression patients to start worrying about things or people they don't have to. While feeling low or ineffectual, people suffering from both disorders more often than not fall prey to each other at the same time. Sometimes, one issue triggers the other one, or can appear at the end of one episode. People with depression may overcome their stress and low feelings, but it's very hard for them to also shake off their sense of fear and worry because they are two very different sensations.

One must not make the mistake of thinking that treating one problem is as good as treating the other. These are two separate issues that need to be tackled individually. While treating depression, a patient's anxiety levels and triggers must also be accounted for to ensure a holistic treatment plan is implemented.

# Chapter 9: Physical and Environment Causes of Anxiety

Do you often have this sensation of butterflies moving around within your tummy? Alternatively, you might feel your heart pounding or the heartbeats going irregular. Then again, you might feel the need to seek a toilet more and more frequently than you did before. Other symptoms include rapid breathing, feeling dizzy, loss of appetite, profuse sweating, etc. All the signs mentioned above indicate just one thing. You are a chronic worrier!

Now, it is quite normal to experience occasional anxiety. Unexpected challenges do crop up in our day-to-day lives. However, they are resolvable too. However, if you are the type, who allows the mind to become so clouded that it stops thinking clearly, then you need help. True, there are professionals around, but you would do better to seek out the root causes of your condition and treat yourself. Let us explore the physical and environmental contributors towards your condition.

**Physical Causes of Anxiety**

There could be several reasons for your anxious responses to stressful situations at home, work or within the community.

## Past and Present Health Status

If you have been feeling unwell for a long time, have nagging pain or have a general feeling of unease, it is time to visit a medical practitioner. However, you are terribly frightened about what you might hear when you get to a clinic/hospital! It is obvious that something is seriously wrong with you, and you have refused to acknowledge it thus far. Naturally, the anxiety continues to build up. It becomes worse after you undergo all kinds of tests and receive a final diagnosis. For instance, you could be having cancer or a tumor in your body. Even if it is benign in nature, you cannot help feeling that you are going to die. Therefore, the status of your health can prove to be a significant factor in causing deep anxiety. This is because it links to the immediate production of personal feelings. True, regular consultations thereafter, as well as psychotherapy can be beneficial in helping you take charge of your emotions. Nonetheless, you cannot rid yourself of worry, for you are always wondering what will happen next.

In actuality, it is difficult for you, or for anyone else, to accept a change in normal health status. For example, if you were to suffer from chronic illnesses, such as coronary artery disease, cardiovascular conditions, diabetes, hyperthyroidism, hypothyroidism, respiratory disorders, etc, you would go through each day with trepidation. After all, these conditions are acute or chronic, and can even turn life threatening some day. It does not help that you have to keep monitoring your weight, food habits, lifestyle, etc, all the time, either. The result is more anxiety, especially if some members of your immediate or extended family are also suffering. You knew that you were susceptible, but did feel that you would be the lucky one escaping from such horrible situations!

Life can become even more difficult if you have to force yourself to tolerate an acutely painful condition. It could be arthritis, irritable bowel syndrome, fibromyalgia, etc. Sometimes, you have the misfortune to become the victim of a rare condition. To illustrate, rare tumours may show up, which encourage the adrenal glands to produce more cortisol. Therefore, every time you encounter a challenge, you keep wondering whether you can muster up sufficient courage to fight it or not. Alternatively, you give yourself no choice at all, but just step aside to let things take their course. Naturally, your stress levels are always on the higher side.

Then again, you may seek relief in illicit substances, anti-anxiety medications or alcohol, to cover up your own inadequacies or worries. For some time, at least, you feel strong and brave. However, as soon as the effects of the drug, medication or alcohol wear off, you return to your highly anxious state of mind. Therefore, you take recourse to these 'treatments' once again. Thus, it is a vicious cycle of consumption and withdrawal. Even complete withdrawal can evoke symptoms of anxiety.

Sometimes, the heightened anxiety is due to the presence of an anxiety disorder itself! You wonder why you should suffer when all your blood relatives have escaped. Then again, you have never run away from circumstances or situations just because you suffered from excessive anxiety. Therefore, how could you have an anxiety disorder? The self-torture is more as you ponder over your peaceful childhood with no worries. The sudden advent of so much anxiety during adulthood seems difficult to accept.

### OTC and Prescription Drugs

Specific over-the-counter or OTC drugs, or even certain prescription medications, have ingredients that cause symptoms of anxiety. They are active in nature, inducing feelings of unease and discomfort. These drugs include medicines dealing with cough and congestion, birth control pills and drugs for weight loss. The worry over what is happening within your body can reach such a level that you are on the verge of collapse.

### Skipping Meals

Glucose is the fuel that keeps your bodily systems functioning. If you lose track of your meals on a regular basis, you will suffer. As your blood-sugar levels drop below normal, a growling tummy and nervous hands produce feelings of anxiety. Hunger is responsible for mood swings, agitation, nervousness and anxiety. Therefore, carry healthy snacks with you wherever you go.

## Over dependence on Caffeine

Are you addicted to coffee or other caffeinated beverages? Do you use them as pick-me-ups throughout the day, simply because you have to be alert at work? If yes, they can prove to be trigger factors for anxiety attacks. Caffeine makes your nervous system even more nervous! People suffering from social anxiety disorder or panic disorder will testify to the same.

## Alteration in Brain Structure

Genes can cause alterations in brain structure. So, can traumatic/stressful experiences. With the alteration in structure, the brain's functioning also undergoes a change. Therefore, there is disruption in the quantities of hormonal secretions. Even the electric signals undergo disturbances. Thus, the brain becomes extremely sensitive to trigger factors of anxiety.

## Environmental Causes of Anxiety

Even the immediate or external environment can prove stressors for a sensitive individual.

## Travel Stress

Does this sound unbelievable? Even if it does, it is perfectly true! Many people lose control over their emotions as they travel long distances to work day-after-day. You could be one of them too. For instance, you could be residing in the suburbs, or even in the countryside. Unfortunately, your workplace is quite far away. Encountering small and large traffic jams along the way can make you feel that you are going mad! You even wonder why no one can drive as well as you do, for then there would be no traffic jams! Alternatively, you may be driving to a railway station and then getting onto a train for travelling to work. If you keep missing your train often, your employer is not going to be very happy with you. Over time, you become a victim of chronic stress, followed by chronic anxiety. Even your physical health is bound to suffer.

Sometimes, your job involves frequent travel. You are eternally rushing to meet people and adhere to fixed schedules. It is as if you are living your life out of a suitcase. Sometimes, you have no time properly. You have to survive on junk food. The lack of good, home-cooked meals or nutritious menus can lead to health issues. Then again, you may be sleep deprived, or having to adjust to different time zones often. This is stressful too. Have you had to travel to places located at high altitudes sometimes? If yes, you might have suffered from heart palpitations, headache and dizziness, breathlessness, etc. These symptoms are similar to those witnessed in panic attacks or severe anxiety attacks. The culprit is altitude. You feel the lack of sufficient oxygen, and therefore,

your body responds to this stress anxiously. If you
had to sleep at these altitudes, you would find
yourself suffering from insomnia or disturbed sleep.
Fortunately, these anxiety attacks, or even panic
attacks, are generally temporary in nature.
Later on, habits like smoking, consuming of illicit
substances or drinking may creep into your life.
Once you become addicted, it is difficult to let go.
You should not be surprised to see anxiety
disorders become an integral part of your life!

**Stress at Workplace**

There is no guarantee that even if you reach your
office on time, you will have a peaceful time every
day. After all, people with different mindsets have
come together onto a common platform. There are
bound to be conflicts at times. They can take the
form of mild disagreements, which are easily
resolved via the intervention of a third party. They
can take the form of intense arguments, wherein
even third party intervention does not work.
Problems with maintaining cordial or respectful
relationships tend to arise. The individual from the
other party could be your co-worker, a team
member, business partner or an employer.
Conflicts tend to leave a bad taste in the mouth! If
you are a hypersensitive individual, you may
continue to brood over what happened long after
everything was over. This brooding takes on a
vicious form. In fact, you continue to expect the
worst from the workplace each day. Even if others
are arguing in front of you, your muscles bunch up

in tension. Thus, you invite acute anxiety into your life. Unless you talk with someone, you will continue to suffer.

## At Public Places

It could be that you have always been a very quiet person. You prefer to do your work in silence. You talk only when there is a need to do so. It follows, therefore, that you find it hard to converse confidently with your employer or other senior members of the organisation. Therefore, if someone were to ask you to make a public presentation, read a report aloud, participate in a competition, etc, you would be terrified out of your wits! In fact, right from the day that you received your order until the day of the display, you would be unable to think or sleep.

It is the same at social events. You cannot always escape attending them. However, you get into a cold sweat, every time you think of walking into a room filled with strangers. You wonder what you will say to people and how you will interact with anybody. Therefore, office parties, social events, etc, create heightened anxiety in your mind.

## Negative Mindset

If you prefer to avoid crowds or meet people, it indicates that you do not have too much of confidence in yourself. As everybody else is, you possess average intelligence and specific talents too.

However, hardly anyone gets to see them, or even understand you as a person. They cannot, for your mind rules over your body (actions). Your mind is a storehouse of negative thoughts and feelings. It cannot help itself for the words you utter to yourself when you are angry, frustrated or upset, are terrible! You consider yourself inferior to others, and even envy them for the way they present themselves to the rest of the world. However, you cannot bring yourself to treat them as inspiring models and emulate their actions. Thus, you remain anxious about your performance, your behaviour, etc, always.

**Financial Worries**

Chronic anxiety loves to target people beset by financial concerns. Therefore, if you find yourself in deep debt, you will always remain in a state of fearful anxiety. There is the fear of going to prison too! Similarly, if your income and expenditure remain equal to one another, you find yourself with no savings. Here, fears about the future or thoughts about retirement will worry you to death!
Now, this is not a common occurrence, but sometimes, personal triggers are the culprit. However, you may not be able to identify them yourself. A professional may have to do the needful and prescribe treatment. One example is post-traumatic stress disorder (PTSD), which follows traumatic events that occurred in the past. It could have a link to bad memories.

# Chapter 10: How to get rid of Anxiety

It might astound you to know that anxiety can be good for you too! For instance, it can teach you to be careful or cautious. Imagine yourself crossing a busy street. Will you not look to the left and right, and wait for speeding vehicles to pass by, before you move one-step ahead at a time? Then again, will you not look at your surroundings prior to walking down a dark alley/street? In simple language, anxiety helps you to stay alive! Similarly, feeling anxious about meeting deadlines, worrying about children's safety, concern about areas of pain in your body, etc, are normal.

However, the same feelings of anxiety can prove worrisome, if they become too intense. To illustrate, you are often on the edge, believing that the worst will always happen. The symptoms that will show up include irritability, constant fatigue, sleeplessness, etc. You may even experience panic attacks or withdraw yourself from society.

Now, the easiest way out is to request someone else to treat your condition. However, you will do better if you treat yourself via the handy tips outlined below.

## Tips to get rid of anxiety

### Acceptance

Yes, it is imperative that you accept the fact that you are a chronic worrier. Do not go around, saying,

"Everybody feels anxious some time or the other. How am I different from them?" You are different because even the flimsiest of things tend to make you nervous and frightened! By accepting your problem, you take the first step towards strengthening your weak mindset.

## Belly Breathing

Deep breathing or belly breathing does calm the mind. Furthermore, it is easy to handle. To begin with, find a comfortable and quiet place, where you will remain undisturbed. Sit down on a floor mat, cross-legged. Alternatively, occupy a chair. Keep your back straight, yet, the spine and shoulders relaxed. Close your eyes.
After a couple of minutes or so, direct your attention towards your nose and nostrils. Place one hand on your stomach. Place the other on your chest. This will help you sense your breathing, as air enters and exits your body. Now, inhale deeply, albeit slowly. Use a count of four to stay on track. Hold your breath, again in alignment with a count of four. Release your breath slowly, mentally counting from 1-4. The hand on your chest will move outwards, while that on the belly will move inwards, during inhalation. The reverse happens during exhalation. True, thoughts will pour in, in order to disturb your concentration. Well, make an effort to drag your attention back to your breathing. It would be good to engage in belly breathing every single day. The ideal time would be in the morning. Of course, there is no restriction on repeating the

exercise twice or thrice during the day too. Maybe, you could go in for two or three shifts, each of 15 minutes duration. Over time, due to regular practice, you will learn to live in the present, and not think about the past or future.

**Exercise**

Physical activity can never harm! Every member of the medical fraternity agrees with this! Therefore, make exercise a part of your daily routine. Your nerves will thank you for it! Of course, the intensity may vary in alignment with health status and age. Whatever you do, your mind will acquire sharper clarity. You will sleep better at night, thanks to lessening of anxiety. Best of all, the brain increases the release of endorphins. They are neurochemicals (chemicals that influence the functioning of the nerves and nervous system), which lessen pain. In other words, they will aid in initiating positive thoughts and making you feel happier. Thus, exercise your way to physical, mental, emotional and spiritual health!

**Dietary Regimen**

Surprisingly, certain foods and beverages tend to enhance feelings of anxiety! For instance, are you addicted to soda? It does not matter whether you drink it in small/large quantities. The corn syrup containing high levels of fructose will not benefit your bodily systems. The other ingredients in the soda are of no use either. They deprive your body of essential minerals and vitamins. Then again, soda destroys your teeth. To illustrate, the minerals in the outer layers begin to lessen. Therefore, your teeth become more vulnerable to the formation of cavities. The same thing happens when your saliva becomes less acidic in nature. Above all, soda does not allow the central nervous system (brain, spinal cord and nerves originating from the spine) to function as well as it should.

Sugar is great for enhancing anxiety. It can even lead to sudden panic attacks. This is because it weakens your mind's abilities to deal with stress. As a result, you end up feeling slow, low and sluggish. Sugar stimulates the fight/flee glands in your body – the adrenal glands. Therefore, you may experience aggression coupled with anxiety, or fear combining with anxiety. However, if you go to the other extreme of not having sugar at all, this will cause harm too. You will sense the adverse effect in the form of heart palpitations.

Too much of caffeinated beverages are excellent triggers for anxiety/panic attacks too! They induce palpitations in your heart. Another thing that you must avoid is processed foods. Wheat and products prepared from refined flour are responsible for inflammation. Finally, there are food allergies. You may not even be aware if you have any. However, if they are present, they will put your nervous system into overdrive!

Therefore, what is the solution?

Obviously, you will need to adhere to a balanced and healthy dietary regimen. For example, you may bring the Go Green concept to your dining table too! Every morning, consume a glass of 'green' juice. You may use green and leafy vegetables, green apples, cucumber, green limes, etc, as ingredients. Apart from this, opt for a breakfast, which is rich in protein. Of course, your body must obtain its quota of carbohydrates too. Therefore, go in for foodstuffs possessing complex carbohydrates. An example is whole grains. They will keep your weight down too. Then again, ensure that you consume plenty of water throughout the day. In case, you are fond of alcohol, strive to limit your consumption. If possible, eliminate it from your life! Why are we emphasizing so much on adopting healthy dietary regimens?

Unhealthy foods stimulate the secretion of the cortisol hormone in your body. Therefore, if your stress levels are already on the higher side, cortisol tends to worsen the situation. Your hidden feelings of anxiety, depression or irritability come to the fore. Anxiety prevents proper digestion of food too. Regardless, depression or anxiety tends to create a craving for food. In turn, this can lead to weight gain. Other effects include loss of sleep, inflammation or lessening of energy levels. Therefore, if you desire to keep your cortisol levels under control, opt for specific plants renowned as adaptogenic herbs. They improve your bodily and mental responses to stressors in the environment. A few examples of these herbs are holy basil, rosemary, liquorice root, milk thistle, Asian ginseng, Ginseng eleuthero and Rhodiola rosa. No, you do not have to hunt for them anywhere. Several online and offline stores stock them in the form of powders and liquids. Be cautious about quantity, though. Request an experienced herbalist or a medical practitioner to help you. These herbs may cause adverse reactions or side effects, if you are on other medications. The same thing is possible if you are pregnant or a nursing mother. Foods containing vitamin C in large quantities are great stress busters too. Towards this end, make grapefruits, berries (blackberries, strawberries, blueberries and raspberries), tomatoes, oranges, papayas, red and green peppers, guavas, Brussels' sprouts, kale and broccoli, essential inclusions in your diet. In fact, you may combine small portions of adaptogenic herbs with vitamin C-rich vegetables/fruits.

**Lavender Oil**

Even practitioners of aromatherapy consider it a favourite! It has such soothing properties! For instance, anxiety causes tense muscles. Well, just give your skin a wonderful massage with lavender oil and watch how your muscles lose their knots! Alternatively, sprinkle a couple of drops of the oil into your bath water. Immerse yourself in the bathtub for some time, and experience the difference. All the pain from your aching muscles and joints disappears quickly!
Anxiety can lead to frequent headaches. Place a few drops of lavender oil onto a soft cotton ball, or even on your fingertips. Massage your temples. The

pleasant smell itself will suffice to relieve an aching head. Similarly, you may add a couple of drops to a tissue. Place this tissue under the pillow at night. The smell will usher you into dreamland quickly!

## Sleep-Wake Cycle

No, you cannot allow yourself to become sleep deprived at all, if you are keen to rid yourself of anxiety. To illustrate, you work late hours because of your nervousness about meeting deadlines or inclination towards submitting perfect work. The next day, your brain quickens its responses to events and situations, without giving itself much time to thicken. They are anticipatory responses that do not give much importance to logic. Therefore, get into the habit of sleeping and waking up at particular times, every day. If your sleep-wake cycle is healthy, you will be relaxed throughout the day and night. However, this will not happen if you fail to manage your 24 hours wisely. It would help if you prepare a list of things to do for the next day, the previous night itself. This way, you will remember all the tasks that you have to take to completion. Over time, you will stop rushing around!
Another aspect that comes in the way of attaining undisturbed sleep is addiction to television, computer or Smart phone. Their screens emit blue light. If your eyes receive this light in moderation, there is no harm. However, overexposure can contribute towards a disturbance in your sleep-wake cycle. Sleep deprivation, in turn, will lead to

daytime tiredness and drowsiness. It follows that your anxiety levels will touch a new high! Therefore, stay away from digital devices/gadgets/appliances at least half-an-hour or so prior to bedtime. Do not even place your Smart phone near your bed!

**Documentation**

This is such a simple solution to the problem of anxiety that it does not receive the attention it deserves! Yes, simple documenting of your negative emotions and thoughts suffice to destroy them! To illustrate, whenever you feel that you cannot cope any more, grab a paper and pen. Write down exactly what you are thinking or feeling at that moment. Do not worry about vocabulary, language or grammar. Just be honest in your outpourings. Once you are through, tear up the sheets of paper without reading what you have written. You will be surprised at how light you feel! This is catharsis or purging of emotional tensions. Once you find yourself in a calmer frame of mind, give some thought to 'reality' as it exists. Make a comparison between imagined thoughts and real situations. True, you may not find it so easy to be objective, because of your lack of self-confidence, self-esteem, etc. Regardless, do not stop trying. When you compare the reality with your core beliefs, you may find that you have been worrying for nothing. To illustrate, it could be that you had been hankering after a prized promotion for quite some time. Unfortunately, it went to someone else. Well, view your past performance from a third person's point of view. Had your employer been partial, or was the loss your own fault? What can you do to improve your position in future?

Do make recording of feelings and thoughts plus comparison with reality, a daily habit. Then, you will understand how vivid your imagination has always been! Thus, you will be able to replace negativity with positivity.

These are just a few ideas; there are several more. For instance, you may go in for regular de-cluttering. Similarly, you may plan leisure activities. Join a support group. Above all, practice gratitude. Be grateful for all your blessings, and stop cribbing about what you do not have!

# Chapter 11: The Drug-Free Therapy for throwing anxiety out of your life

Treating illnesses that do not have physical causes is most often thought to be unnecessary, or something that can be done easily. Most people also think that disorders such as anxiety can be overcome over a period of time without doing anything much except may be going out with friends for a drink or going on a vacation.

The truth is, clinical anxiety disorder patients are not the only ones who should worry about handling their stress better. There is a vast majority of people who are unaware of their condition in the first place. An ever bigger population of those are too occupied with paying their bills, trying to fit in a round of exercises, working, and family to think about treating something as intangible as anxiety. Some of us may have been anxious right from a small age while some may have developed anxiety disorders as they became older. Irrespective of when the problem started, people need to ensure it gets treated once properly and fully diagnosed. Such people are usually suffering from a hyperactive mind and are always worried that they will lose their firm grasp on life and sanity.

The most common and easiest way to tackle anxiety, for many, many years has been simply popping pills. But these pills have a very high price, sometimes more than just in terms of money. Some of these pills have drastic side effects such as decreased libido, excessive hunger, and insomnia just form the tip of the iceberg.

There is good news for people who want to ditch the chemical route and opt for healthier alternatives instead. There are actually better ways to conquer fears and getting their nerves under control.

**The Drug-free Therapy**

Here are some of the simple ones listed for you:

### 1. Express it Loud

Expressing your anxiety and emotions to someone you can trust is very therapeutic indeed. But even better than talking about such things calmly is to actually yell them out at the top of your lungs. Usually as kids, we are reprimanded for yelling and shouting without thinking about those around us. But that rule doesn't always have to be followed by adults. If you're frustrated or have pent-up regressive emotions, then let it rip.

By this, it doesn't imply that you should express violently such that other people are afraid of you or put on edge. This is more about a health way of expressing yourself in a controlled environment. The more you try to suppress these feelings, the more it can take you under instead. What you need to do is embrace your anxiety as a part of your life and then let go of it. Find an empty room and yell at the top of your lungs when required, punch a pillow, stomp your feet, or simply mash the first of one of your hands into the palm o the other. Even these little outlets go a long way in reducing your anxiety levels.

A yoga instructor in Los Angeles had even setup a class known with "Tantrum Yoga" included. In this, you are encouraged to use unconventional methods in order to release the negativities that are lodged in our body and can get converted into diseases and stress.

## 2. Step up your Pace

People who tend to shut themselves from the world prefer not to do anything remotely active, although their mind is racing all over the place. The few who think about making an attempt at exercising may perhaps get daunted at the thought of having sore muscles post workout or extreme fatigue. Some people may jump straight to the work case scenario and worry about exercising so much that they suffer a stroke or a cardiac arrest. But the truth is exercising is the best way to tackle anxiety. It's natural, inexpensive, and works wonders. All it takes is determination.

There is a scientific reason behind this. Exercising is known to release endorphins and serotonin – the two hormones responsible for making you feel upbeat and happy. People who feel happy on the inside always work harder to improve their life's circumstances on the outside. Apart from keeping you physically fit and affecting your mind positively, exercising also keeps your mind occupied rather than letting it wander into negative thoughts again. The goal should be to put in a minimum of 30 minutes every day at least 5 days a week. This doesn't necessarily have to include painful workouts at the gym. It can be something as simple as doing some yoga right in your room, walking around your apartment blocks, or simply dancing to your favorite tunes.

### 3. Eliminate Caffeine

A cup of cocoa, hot chocolate, or coffee and tea can actually prove to be beneficial to your body. But if you rely on a hit of caffeine every time you are stressed, then you've got a problem on your hands and in your bloodstream.
Caffeine works like an electric shot on your system and helps in boosting energy levels substantially instantly. But because of this, simmering worry or simple nervousness can actually get blown into a full blown panic attack. Some people break out in a sweat at the thought of giving up their continuous supply of caffeine, much like a drug addict who is asked to abstain from their favourite drug forever. But thankfully with caffeine, you don't have to give it up entirely. The key is to consume safe levels of it every day so that it benefits rather than causing harm.
People who chug down unlimited cups of coffee can switch to 2 regular sized cups of coffee a day. And regular size here refers to 8 ounces, nothing more than that. So if you're saying on 6 ups as of now, try to reduce one cup the first week, and then the next cup over the next week. By doing this gradually,

you're not causing your body to react violently on the loss of a stimulant but rather adapt to lower levels of it.

## 4. Gift Yourself some Bedtime

In today's world, people are either busy with a hectic personal or professional schedule, or they are too busy with the thoughts crowding their head to worry about sleeping. Yes, you read that right. Sleep is the best gift we can give ourselves, no matter we tell ourselves. For those who brag of sleeping just 3-4 hours every day and still function normally – they don't know they're just a moving, breathing ticking bomb. Don't listen to what others or what your own anxieties tell you. You need to sleep adequately every day in order to overcome your anxiety issues.

Not many people know this but depriving your mind and body of rest will surely cause anxiety, at the minimum, in the long run. No matter what label you give yourself or what you're struggling with, anxiety will catch up if you don't work on getting enough sleep. Insomniacs, self-professed night owls, or over achievers increase the chances of remaining actively anxious at all times without even knowing when they're doing it. By sleeping for at least 8-9 nine hours, uninterrupted, you're not just doing yourself a favour, but even those around you. One of the best ways to try and fall asleep, if you find that tough, is to take a book to bed. It can be any bed – a journal, a novel, or a biography, but reading in bed is known to promote easy drifting into sleep. But do bear in mind that you need to take books and not electronic gadgets like mobiles and laptops to bed. Apart from books, ding simple things like deep breathing exercises or meditating for 10-15 minutes help with falling asleep, all without pills.

### 5. It's Okay to Say No

There is only so much you can do, tolerate or listen to. Try doing anything beyond that for a long time, and you feel your restraints slipping, and anxiety seeping in. If people add their own baggage on top of your own issues, then there is only so much of it you can take. While it is good to give more than receive, this rule doesn't hold good for being dumped on repeatedly with others issues. Not only they eat into time that you can gift yourself, but impositions made by others on you can also add to your own frustration, feel helpless and perpetually guilty. These emotions, singly or as a combination, will force you to step out of your comfort zone repeatedly and put our own mind and body at risk. Small things, like running errands for others, paying their bills for them, tiding them over with some spare cash once in a while, or letting them lean on your shoulder or simply listening to their problems by lending your ear is all good when you do it in moderation without putting yourself at risk. After taking care of them and their problems, there is very little strength to take care of yourself, and even lesser motivation to do so sometimes. Who will take care of you, your affairs and problems when the time arrives? Well, it can't be anyone else; it has to always be you first.

So does this mean you should stop helping people or being kind to them? Certainly not. But what it means is that you learn your limits. Anything beyond that, learn to say no and ensure your choices are respected. Don't be afraid of saying no and walking away when your needs and choices are not cared for.

### 6. Have All, Wholesome Meals

People struggling with anxiety usually also experience bouts of nausea. At these times, the thought of eating anything is far from appealing. The downside of this issue though is that without food, your body reacts in a more negative manner, this worsening the issue. Due to lack of a regular food schedule, our body starts producing higher levels of the hormone cortisol, or also known as the stress hormone. While small levels of cortisol are actually beneficial to help you keep your wits about during challenging times, very high levels of the same hormone can trigger anxiety attacks.

While it is necessary for you to eat, what also matters is eating at regular intervals and food which improves your health. Some people think that eating their favourite foods will always do the trick. They will feel happier, ergo anxiety takes a backseat. While this may hold good for a short amount of time, poor food choices are also known to create hormonal imbalances, which of course worsen any psychological problems. So let's not use anxiety as an excuse to binge eat junk food loaded with grease, sugar, artificial colours, and below-par ingredients.

People who are always on the edge, for example experience dizzying sugar rushes when they eat or drink something that is loaded with excessive amounts of sugar. These include visible physical symptoms such as shaking and breaking out in a sweat. Some may mistake these to be symptoms of a panic attack, and this worry will actually cause that which you were just obsessing over until then. There are actually healthy foods that are good for both mind and body. Adding more lean meats, fruits, vegetables, and sources of healthy fats will do wonders to your physical health and improve your mental health too. It is recommended that one eats small portions of healthy food, or throw in a healthy shake or smoothie in between, 5-6 times a day. Refined carbs and sugar should be avoided as much as possible.

### 7. Have an Exit Strategy

Not all circumstances in life can be predicted, much less controlled by us. There will be times when you can only watch the events play out before you and do nothing about them. For people with anxiety issues, this can be a very challenging time, especially if they run into a rough patch in life, or even find themselves in uncomfortable situations. It is thus important for you to have an exit strategy, a backup plan that you can fall back on when things don't go your way. For example, there is a family emergency because of which you have to interact with a few people whom you usually avoid because they bully you. Because you cannot avoid being with your family during a difficult time, you can instead always keep yourself with activities that will keep you as far away from them as possible and minimize the number of encounters with them. Try to be around people whom you love and trust so they don't get an opportunity to harass you. But the best exit strategy? Simply find ways to stand up to them or beat them at their own game.

# Chapter 12: Meditation as the Way to Heal Yourself

People suffering from chronic illnesses or recovering from sudden traumatic experiences usually receive post operative treatments, such as counselling and physiotherapy. In addition to these, doctors also recommend their patients to indulge in a little bit of meditation to heal sooner. Some people have raved about the benefits of meditation because they claim it helped them heal faster. Others are simply relieved to put aside their worries and pains for some time and simply sit in peace and quiet. No matter what the degree of impact is, meditation has helped several people struggling with various forms of pains.

When meditation can prove to be so beneficial for the aches of the body, don't you think it can also benefit people struggling with the pains of their mind and heart? After all, meditation is mainly related to controlling your mind – putting it at ease and enforcing a sense of calmness.

Some people meditate simply because it's a part of their culture, or a practice they've adopted and really enjoyed over the past few years. There are those who have embraced meditation in order to heal themselves. This form of meditation, known as healing meditation, also incorporates certain visualization techniques. One of the major successes of therapeutic meditation has been observed in handling anxiety.

Some of the simplest forms of visual meditation can be to visualize your mind wearing the brightest hat that you have and walking out of a dark room, confidently and purposefully. This kind of visual meditation will enforce upon your mind that it too can shake itself of its shackles and walk out free and happy.

**Preparing for Healing Meditation**

Some people often confuse meditation with yoga, and get worried about not getting into the right yoga pose or not having all the clothes & equipment for a yoga session. While yoga is a whole different beautiful process altogether, meditation only forms a part of it. So don't worry about complex poses or requirements. The easiest way for you to spend some quality time in meditation is to:

1. Find a quiet spot lacking disruptions or frequent visits from other people
2. Dim lights or turn on simple candles if they help you better
3. Turn off every single gadget near you
4. Sit on a straight back chair, feet down, with your hands palms down on your thighs and head leaning a little in front. Those comfortable sitting with their legs folded in a lotus position can also adopt that pose too. People who cannot go wither either of these options can also life on their backs on the

floor, but not on the bed because then you'll fall asleep rather than meditating.

5. Chant any mantra of your choice slowly and steadily. It can be any healing mantra, something as simple as "Om" too

6. Close your eyes while meditating, and keep your mind as blank as possible. If you cannot blank it out, train your mind to focus on a single point and remain focused on it throughout

**Meditation Mixed with Action**

Not many people can imagine any form of meditation that doesn't have you sitting on the floor, legs folded and eyes closed. These is another, more active way of meditating. Some people can meditate even while performing simple, routine activities like walking or swimming. What is important is that you eliminate all distractions and focus only on the next step or stroke that you will make. This helps keep your mind anchored in the now, the present, and eliminate all stressful thoughts. By focusing on the way you walk, swim, or breathe evenly while performing these activities, you are in fact performing a form of meditation. Some of the other traditional methods of meditation while in action include yoga and Chinese movement therapies such as tai chi and qigong.

## Meditation Techniques to Adopt

### 1. Light, Healing Meditation

For this form of meditation, one must firstly locate a quiet space or room. The next step is to clear your mind as much as possible of your anxieties and quieten your mind. Once you feel yourself relaxing a bit, adopt the pose in which you would like to meditate, close your eyes and imagine a bright light burning behind your eyes.

Focus on the light until there is nothing but the light in your mind's eye. Enjoy the feeling of being alone and at peace with a shining source of light. Then allow yourself feel that light pass all over your body, inch by inch, and imagine it is healing your mind and body of its troubles.

This form of meditation requires patience, and needs to be done slowly so you feel every muscle in your body relax and eliminate anxiety completely.

### 2. Self-visualization Meditation

We know that we ought to dress for the job that we want to do. Similarly, we need to visualize ourselves in our best possible version to be able to know exactly what our aim is.

In a quiet room, when you have calmed your mind sufficiently, picture yourself doing the things that you like or at a position that you have always wanted to be at. Picture yourself doing positive fun activities, reaching your goals, and being a health version of yourself which your anxiety is preventing you from getting at. Try to keep this visualization as realistic as possible because this will trick your mind into believing it more easily, and therefore work towards it with more ease.

With this form of meditation, you are more in sync with your deepest desires. You learn more about yourself and what you want, without the obscuring clouds of anxiety. Once you know what you mind is really longing for, you will find it easier to try to do positive thing to reach your self-defined destination.

### 3. Consider Yourself a Healing Machine

When your mind is at ease, it tends to wander to negative or mischievous plots more easily than landing on a positive platform. Knowing that you are suffering from anxiety should not prevent you from thinking that you can beat this problem. When you think of yourself of a strong, powerful force with enough willpower to heal your mind, your body will automatically work to match what your mind is thinking.

Understand that your body's natural instincts are to remain at an optimum level at all times, to heal with it is damaged, and prevent further damages. Reinforcing positive affirmations and thinking of your body & mind as self-repairing, capable machines will encourage them to behave in a similar fashion. This may take time, but it will happen. Considering your body and mind irreparable because of your anxiety issues is counterproductive to any healing process your mind or body attempt to do instinctively.

## 4. Remapping your Brain's Wires

Dr. Richard Davidson, Director of the Laboratory for Affective Neuroscience, University of Wisconsin, performed an interesting study involving meditating monks and brainwaves. What he found is that the circuitry of a monk's brain is quite different from that of an average, common man who doesn't meditate on a regular basis.

When a normal person is confronted with triggers like anxiety, fear, anger, and depression, the amygdala and right prefrontal cortex of the brain become very active. When the meditating monks faced similar situations, a different part of their brain became active. Rather than the parts of the brain already mentioned getting activated, their left prefrontal cortex had more activity. This part of the brain is responsible for making us feel happy and positive. It doesn't mean that the monks failed to recognize the challenges for what they were. The difference was due to their longer duration of remaining happy, a more positive part of their brain became engaged to tackle adverse situations in a positive manner.

This discovery led to another one. Until a few years back, doctors believed that a person's brain was wired or "pre-set" in a particular manner. With this study however, they were able to prove that by following positive or negative habits, a person can re-map their brain and change their general perspective to everything in life. People's natural instincts to respond in a situation or handle an obstacle can be altered by long periods of meditations.

For people suffering with anxiety, this is groundbreaking discovery because it means a person doesn't have to be enslaved to their shortcomings but there are ways in which they can control it to a large extent, if not overcome the challenges they represent fully.

# Chapter 13: How to Feel Good

Many people often think that achieving a particular goal or accumulating immeasurable wealth is the way to being happy. A few others believe that only when a certain person is in their lives, or if they are surrounded by people who always agree to everything they say, they can be truly happy and at peace with everyone. What is essential to note here is that all the sources of happiness in these cases lies on the outside, on other people. Not on the person who wants to be happy.

We set ourselves small & big goals to define the moment when we think we would be happy. They could be as simple as:

1. If I could get my favourite cup of coffee this morning without having to wait in a line at the local cafe then I would reach office on time
2. If I could save enough money, I could buy that car that I've been dreaming about for the past year
3. If my co-worker doesn't stop talking about me behind my back to my boss, I think I'm going to lose it!
4. If I get that annual bonus, then I could go on a vacation to my favourite beaches outside town

We spend years and years trying to achieve our

dreams, not realizing the anxiety we put ourselves through. In the absence of our happiness, we don't maintain positive feelings but instead succumb to anger and despair. But there are smart and hardworking people who get what they want eventually. They may wake up 20 minutes earlier so they can get to their coffee shop when it's a little emptier so they don't have to pray for it to be empty. Or they may start working extra hours or better to get a bonus and save enough to buy a car that's not flashy as the original choice but still makes them happy. Or they may have had an open chat with their nasty, backstabbing colleague to set their expectations clearly and nip the problem at its bud. But even after all this, are often not "happy". They instead feel tired, angry or anxious often. Here's why.

Blindly pursuing your dreams without thinking of the toll its having on you and the people you care about will leave you feeling empty and frustrated even after you've been on your dream vacation thrice. The smallest things, like a person texting and walking slowly in front of you can set you off. If you are already experiencing such irritations or anxiety, then it's time for you to step back and re-consider the factors you think are making you happy.

You will find that most, if not all the reasons for your happiness and unhappiness lie on the outside. The problem with focusing on the outside is that you lose focus on what's happening within you, your mind, your body, your spirit. You "hoard" on the reasons to make you happy without first rearranging your own thoughts and feelings in the right manner.

3-Steps to Being Happy

A simple 3-step process to being happy is

1. Thoughts are powerhouses
2. Reflect and interact with your thoughts
3. Choose which emotions you should act on

Let's look at an example of when you are confronted with a challenging situation, say a person talking loudly over the phone right in front of you, in a tiresome long line a government office. The situation is unavoidable – you've already spent 45 minutes in the line and you need to get the work done the same, but you also need to tolerate the guy in front of you. The situation would play out somewhat like this.

Your first reaction would be to think in our mind "this man is so inconsiderate and annoying!" You don't feel comfortable standing behind him and you feel your anxiety levels rising because you're worried about what you'll do if you snap in anger. This constant brooding over the unpleasant situation will lead you to be more angry and yell out in anger – "Hey mister, why speak over the phone to a deaf person who can't hear no mater ho loud you are?!" or "why did I have to be the one stuck in this is super-long line behind you?" or "Why can't the person at the counter work at the speed of a normal human?!" These expressions of anger would of course hurt and possibly anger the object of our anger. You'd have also started feeling heavy and tired of carrying so much anxiety and frustration within you. At this point, what's required is a little empathy. You could direct your mind to think otherwise. "Maybe this guy is speaking to his 90-year old nana after a whole week so he sounds so happy!" or "Maybe he's speaking with his family staying in a different country and the network coverage there must be bad". By thinking such things out of empathy and tolerance you reduce the rush of anger and instead find something nice and warm to contemplate about. This will instantly control your rising anxiety too.

Now that you've harnessed your thoughts, it's time to move to the next step – confronting your emotions and communicating with them. What we perceive certain things to be shape the way we think about them, and thereby respond to them. Our first instinct in this case is to feel anger and annoyance because we perceive the person to be rude and irresponsible, unfeeling of others' feelings. When you have such thoughts, you need to think to reflect on your first thought, on how it may have distorted the facts and how would you respond to the situation rationally instead. So in this case, your thoughts may distract the situation such that you think the other person is misbehaving with you, possible even violent and he has to be reprimanded at all costs. When you talk about to your emotions, you question the validity of that assumption and think that maybe this has nothing to do with respect and violence, and simply poor mobile network. Perhaps the person really is rude in real life, but why should you assume the worst and react poorly to a situation which can instead be ignored or handled in a better way?

Coming to the last bit: create a thought police in your mind who will police your thoughts and what flows to the rest of your body and makes you perform certain actions. Change, when evolutionary, is caused by a reaction or trigger. But when you make changes to the way you think to keep yourself happy, you are in fact changing your entire mental makeup – the easiest way to stay happy at all time and avoid emotions and thoughts that cause you unhappiness instead.

The 3-step process explained above is more of a general workflow that can be implemented to experience more positive thoughts and be happy. But there are several small habits or activities that you can do in order keep that happy mode on at all times.

a. Celebrating small victories – Don't just wait for the big events or achievements in life to feel happy or reward yourself. Instead, look at each small achievement of yours as proof that you are on the way to improving your mental health, to improve the quality of your life.

b. Reach your goal steadily – Rather than trying to make it big or achieving the best possible results in the shortest amount of time, focus on taking small steps to do things that matter the most to you. Sometime, you may feel that your goal is not the right on for you, or can be improved upon. Sometimes, you need to pace things slowly so you don't lose focus or the energy to get to your final destination. Most people are in a hurry to treat anxiety, and they often take the easy way to get there. That's not always the best and safest solution. And when you have new smaller goals on your way to get to claim the biggest prize, you will look at each success as a medal for our efforts.

c. Break large tasks into small parts – Don't bite off more than you can chew. When you know what your limits and capacity are, stick to that and set goals for yourself. Split your work so you can cover it over a period of time so you know each level completed is a success on the right path. Or, if the work needs to be done in a short span of time, split the work among other people.

d. Laugh – it's a simple trick that surprisingly is extremely effective. Make it a habit to laugh rather than grin wryly or look down upon situations in a condescending manner. Laughter is good for your heart and mind.

e. Exercise – Make your mind and body agile so you have that endorphin high to keep your spirits buoyant at all times.

**Other ways to stay happy**

> to approach trust one step at a time, so you know you have someone you can count on
> be trustworthy yourself so people are more inclined to build a relationship with you
> indulge in small pleasures like a spa session or a nice movie night after work
> feel pride in your achievements, making peace with things that you cannot control despite your best efforts
> Dress up nicely just to please yourself and nobody else!
> Clean up your desk at home and office, then your room at home, and then perhaps even your whole house
> Eat your favorite foods from time to time. If they're unhealthy choices – well, a very small portion say twice a month would be a nice reward as well as source of happiness
> Watch funny videos and TV series online or on TV
> Read your favorite books
> And when you feel like crying, go ahead and have a nice, cleansing crying jag without any

hesitation. Sometimes, you need to wash away that old, messy coat of dirt called bad memories and negative emotions from your heart to get a clean, fresh start.

# Chapter 14- Vagus nerve and stimulation of vagus nerve

In scientific terms, the vagus nerve, which was earlier also known as pneumogastric nerve, is one of the nerves found leading from our cranial, or brain region. Also known as CN X in short, this nerve is actually comprised of a pair of nerves, but usually referred to as just one lot. They form a liaison of sorts between our lungs, heart, and digestive system.

The vagus nerves are in fact the longest of all the cranial nerves found in our body. Technically, this nerve is in charge of our inner nerve centre, also known as the parasympathetic nervous system. Because of its control of the inner nervous system, the vagus nerves are also responsible for the most vital functions of our body, such as pumping blood through, the heart, as well as communicating sensory and motor impulses from our brain to the rest of the body. Some of the research conducted in the past few years have established a link between stimulating the vagus nerves and treating chronic inflammation in patients.

**Why is vagus nerves important?**

Here are a few other key reasons why the vagus nerves are so important to us:
1. They prevent inflammation by signaling the brain of the presence of inflammatory

substances in our bodies. The brain in turn causes the release of anti-inflammatory neurotransmitters which guide the body's immune system to target the harmful substances

2. Stimulating the vagus nerves has shown to help people retain memories in a better way. When the nerves are stimulated, a neurotransmitter called norepinephrine was released the amygdala, the part of our brain responsible for retaining memories

3. Properly stimulated vagus nerves helps you breathe in a regular manner because they release the neurotransmitter acetylcholine which instructs our lungs to breathe for us.

4. The vagus nerves also regulate the beating of our heart via electrical pulses

5. Vagus nerves are responsible for dousing the fire lit by our over-active sympathetic nervous system, which is what causes us to react to things, people and situations instinctively. While your first reaction may be to have a panic attack or punch someone in their face, our vague nerves are responsible for the release of acetylcholine which instructs us to remain calm via the release of enzymes and proteins such as oxytocin, vasopressin, and prolactin.

6. Your vagus nerves are responsible for sending your "gut" feeling to your brain, or transmitting your instinctive knowledge via electric impulses known as "action potentials"

Now that we have seen now vital our vagus nerves are, let's see how they can be properly stimulated to improve the lives of people having depressive thoughts or anxiety disorders.
Apart from the invasive and non-invasive vagus nerve stimulation (VNS) procedures commonly prescribed to people with severe forms of depression, there are simpler ways in which even a common man can stimulate the nerve himself. With the medical procedures, the trick is to electrically shock the nerve into functioning properly in a drastic move, when really necessary to be made. Some of the non-invasive treatment procedures can be as simple as giving a wearable device, like a smart phone, to the patient. The device will generate electrical impulses to those regions of our skin where our vagus nerves come into direct contact. Remember, the vagus nerves are also known enteric brain because they access almost every part of our body and act as an extension of the brain itself when impulses have to be communicated to our organs.
With the self-treatment methods, the expectation is more to improve the functioning of the nerve rather than control any serious conditions. The good news for yoga & meditation lovers is that if

you have been practising your breathing exercises regularly, chances are you already have a pretty we stimulated vagus nerve.

## Simulation exercises to try

Just be careful to not over-stress your body when you try these stimulation exercises:

1. Hum – Since the nerve passes from our cranial section all the way down to our body organs, humming or simply chanting "Om" in a slow, long way ensure the vagus nerves "vibrates" without getting agitated. Even humming our favorite tune should do the trick because the process and the results are the same.

2. Regulate your breathing – Consciously focusing on regulating our breathing pattern, an essential part of yoga, goes a long way in energizing our vagus nerves. We usually breathe about 10-14 times a minute. By inhaling, holding your breath to the count of 5, and then exhaling very slowly to the count of 10, we are reducing the number of breaths to about 5-7/minute, but by activating our vagus nerves to function at an optimum level

3. Diving Reflex – Splashing cold water on your face ensuring your lips and tips of your nose and ears are touched also acts as stimulation

because of the nerve ends present at the points. The same effect can also be replicated by placing large cubs of ice and rubbing them all over your face and on the back of your neck. Another method in this technique is to immerse your tongue completely in a mild liquid such as water. Take a sip of lukewarm water, keep it in your mouth for 5-10 seconds, and then sip it slowly. All these small tricks accompanied by deep breathing act immediately in simulating the nerves

4. Valsalva Technique – This is another simple breathing technique in which you gently block your nostrils and also close your nose but force your body to exhale slowly. This activity will create some pressure in your chest activity and thereby activate your vagus nerve.

5. Build connections – The simple act of creating a bond with someone, even by keeping in touch with your loved ones via calls and texts message plays a nourishing role to your vagus nerves by regulating the overall functioning of our mind and body. Even hugging until you relax, which usually takes about 3-4 minutes, is known to have a very uplifting effect on our body and brain.

# Conclusion

Life is not easy – not for you, not for anyone.
Where there is life there is a series of small and
huge struggles each day. But this should be no
reason for anyone to fall prey to depression. This is
your body – your temple of living and you have the
full control of it. Seek help when you cannot do it
alone, but don't let your life go waste; especially if
you know the symptoms of and suspect yourself of
suffering with depression, it is time for some
professional help, not drug overdose to make it go
away. Live life with the respect and love it
deserves – after all, you only live once!